D1605570

Johnny Weissmuller Jr.

TARZAN
My Father

TARZAN

My Father

by
Johnny Weissmuller Jr.
with
William Reed & W. Craig Reed

ECW PRESS

Published by ECW PRESS
2120 Queen Street East, Suite 200, Toronto, Ontario, Canada M4E 1E2

NATIONAL LIBRARY OF CANADA CATALOGUING IN PUBLICATION DATA

Weissmuller, Johnny, 1940–
Tarzan, my father / Johnny Weissmuller Jr., William Reed and W. Craig Reed.

ISBN 1-55022-522-7

1. Weissmuller, Johnny, 1904–1984.
2. Motion picture actors and actresses—United States—Biography.
3. Swimmers—United States—Biography.
I. Reed, William, 1929– . II. Reed, W. Craig. III. Title.

PN2287.W4556W45 2002   791.43'028'092   C2002-902192-8

Copy Editor: Mary Williams
Acquisition Editor: Emma McKay
Production: Erin MacLeod
Design and typesetting: Yolande Martel
Cover design: Guylaine Regimbald – SOLO DESIGN
Printing: Transcontinental
All photos courtesy of the Weissmuller family and Allene Gates McClelland

This book is set in Sabon.

The publication of Tarzan, My Father has been generously supported by the Canada Council, the Ontario Arts Council, and the Government of Canada through the Book Publishing Industry Development Program. Canada

DISTRIBUTION

CANADA: Jaguar Book Group, 100 Armstrong Avenue,
Georgetown, Ontario L7G 5S4

UNITED STATES: Independent Publishers Group, 814 North Franklin Street,
Chicago, Illinois 60610

EUROPE: Turnaround Publisher Services, Unit 3, Olympia Trading Estate,
Coburg Road, Wood Green, London N22 6T2

AUSTRALIA AND NEW ZEALAND: Wakefield Press, 1 The Parade West (BOX 2066),
Kent Town, South Australia 5071

PRINTED AND BOUND IN CANADA

ECW PRESS
ecwpress.com

CONTENTS

Tarzan is a registered trademark of Edgar Rice Burroughs, Inc.

DEDICATION

To my sister Heidi and my wife, Diane. They were, and are, the guardians and the standard-bearers. In their own times, and in their unique ways, they brought and bring honor to the name Weissmuller.

FOREWORD

My grandfather was Edgar Rice Burroughs, the man who created Tarzan. He came to writing late in life, beginning that career when he was thirty-five. He'd been restless in the other professions he'd tried, be it railroad policeman in Idaho or member of the Seventh Cavalry chasing Apaches in the last years of the wild Wild West in the 1800s. Finally, he tried writing, and his third novel was *Tarzan of the Apes*. That was in 1912.

For me, however, the first Tarzan wasn't what my grandfather wrote, because before I could even read I'd seen Tarzan come to life on the movie screen. When I was a small child in the 1940s (my grandfather died in 1950), the family would gather at my grandfather's home on weekends, where he'd screen sixteen-millimeter Tarzan movies, and that's where I first saw Johnny Weissmuller. It was only later that I came to understand that other actors had played Tarzan. As a small child, however, all I knew was that Johnny Weissmuller *was* Tarzan. There was something about him. Even when he was less robust, in the 1940s, he still had a screen presence that commanded your attention. He made us believe in Tarzan.

Looking back now, at both the films and the memorabilia, I can see that in the earliest of his motion pictures, *Tarzan the Ape Man* and *Tarzan and His Mate*, Weissmuller was at his peak. Fresh from his Olympic victories, he—and costar Maureen O'Sullivan—radiated youth, strength, power, and—dare I say it—even beauty. I have a Coca-Cola tray from the early 1930s that features Johnny and Maureen from *Tarzan and His Mate*, and it's a toss-up as to which is the more attractive, because they're both stunning examples of the Hollywood glorification of youth. Leonardo DiCaprio at twenty-two has nothing on Johnny Weissmuller when he was twenty-eight or thirty. DiCaprio should pray that he looks as good at thirty as Johnny Weissmuller did.

There is a mystique that surrounded Johnny Weissmuller, and it followed him all of his life. When he left Tarzan films to play Jungle Jim and other roles, it was as Tarzan that people always remembered him, particularly after the films were revived on television.

Tarzan's call, as immortalized by Johnny Weissmuller, has to be one of the most recognizable sounds on the face of the Earth. Today, that same Tarzan yell is a registered trademark owned by Edgar Rice Burroughs, Inc.

In the 1970s, Johnny attended a gathering of Edgar Rice Burroughs fans in Los Angeles and, standing on a balcony overlooking the hotel lobby, he let loose with the immortal yell. Everyone within earshot stopped what they were doing to look up at him, because they instantly recognized the sound—whether they were hotel clerks, bellhops, or tourists. Moreover, when they saw that it really was him (and not an incredible simulation), they smiled and applauded elatedly.

Johnny Weissmuller became a legend in his own time, and this book is his story as only his son could tell it.

DANTON BURROUGHS,
Secretary, Edgar Rice Burroughs, Inc.

INTRODUCTION

Johnny Weissmuller was universally idolized, both during and after his lifetime. Fans not only adored him as the greatest Olympic champion swimmer of his time, but they also remember him to this day as the greatest Tarzan of them all.

Why? I have asked myself that question many times. In the documentary film *Investigating Tarzan*, George McWhorter, curator of the Burroughs Memorial Collection, Louisville University, Kentucky, suggested that it probably had a lot to do with the times. The more I thought about that, the more I tended to agree.

My father's classic films encompassed the period of the Great Depression in the United States, which started with the Wall Street Crash of 1929. It was not only a national economic depression, but it was also a period of emotional and mental depression for the breadwinners whose families were going without food. They wanted to work; they wanted to provide for their families; they wanted to succeed in life; but there was no work, and there was no way that they could avoid, eventually, the personal shame of the breadline. But for ten or fifteen cents, they could watch Tarzan, Lord of the Apes and lord of his environment, succeed time and time again against all odds. Tarzan was a symbol of hope. Times would get better. They, like Tarzan, would be free and independent men, in charge of their own destinies. As McWhorter commented, "Tarzan is a survivor—Tarzan is a winner—every generation has, and needs, a Tarzan image."

Mark Goodman perhaps sums it up best in an article published in 1984, just after my father's death:

I want to remember Weissmuller as the Tarzan, swift and strong, of those lambent days of my youth, when we would pedal down to the Majestic Theater to watch him perform his jungle wonders. Tarzan called us back to a simpler, primitive world, where right was clean and sharp, and wrong redeemable; where justice could be dispensed with a jungle mandate, a stone-sharpened knife, and a little help from diverse animal friends. Tarzan let us believe that there still exists, somewhere, nature's own knight-errant to catch our children in the rye, and to slay the Beast from the treetops, every blessed Saturday morning.

Tarzan was all of that, but he was more than that. He was also a man, with the strengths and weaknesses of all men. He had a great sense of humor, so much so that Red Skelton once told him that he had missed his calling; he would have made a good stand-up comedian. But, like most stand-up comedians, he also had his dark side. He was a kind man who could at times be cruel. He was an honest man who could at times be deceptive. He was mostly a giver but sometimes a taker. He was a man of peace and a man of conflict. He was optimistic and pessimistic, and he experienced—in the blink of an eye—monumental emotional highs and dramatic lows. In short, he was a lot like the rest of us, although perhaps on a larger scale. Johnny Weissmuller was bigger than life. He reaped more than his share of glory, and he also endured more tragedy than almost any man I have ever known. That's what this book is all about: the glory and the tragedy of Johnny "Tarzan" Weissmuller.

When I was sixteen, Dad took me on a fishing trip to Acapulco, Mexico. While we were being photographed with our catch—two large sailfish—a little Mexican boy no older than nine, who had been staring at us for some time, inquisitively pulled on Dad's pant leg. Dad glanced down at the barefoot boy, who was beaming up at him, his two front teeth missing.

"Perdón señor, ¿Tarzán? ¿Tú eres Tarzán?"

My dad, whose best Spanish was "buenos morning," cocked an eyebrow. "Sí, me Tarzan."

Dad followed this with the famous Tarzan yell, at full throttle. Within minutes, the entire village, now suddenly awake from their afternoon siesta, gathered on the pier, gawking and pointing. For a teenager, this was a thoroughly embarrassing experience, but it made such an impression on me that I never forgot it. You see, my father *believed* he was Tarzan, and so did nearly the entire planet.

Over the years, and especially after Dad's death in 1984, a great store of historical Tarzan and Weissmuller family information and documents came into my possession, including numerous family diaries, letters, and photographs. My wife, Diane, and I collected and preserved a cache of material relating to Johnny Weissmuller. Much of this is quite personal, revealing, and sensitive, which is why we chose, for many years, not to share it with anyone—until now. Several years ago, we made the decision that it was time to tell the world. We simply could not hope to keep the family secrets buried forever—best that they come from us rather than surface in distorted forms in the *National Enquirer*.

We gathered together our boxes of information: newspaper clippings from as long ago as 1922; passports; original birth certificates; private-investigator reports; personal letters; hundreds of family photographs dating back to the late 1800s; scads of printed information, handwritten notes, and even a few tape recordings that I made with my father when I was a young man.

Due to the intimate nature of much of this information, we decided to work with some friends we could trust to write about Johnny Weissmuller's life from a personal perspective and not turn this book into yet another glamorous dissertation on his swimming and film careers, or degrade it into a scandalous "paparazzi" article. I contacted my writer friends, historian-biographer William Reed and his son W. Craig.

William Craig is also a computer-research whiz. Together, we began to make sense of this mountain of historical information. I had no idea that such a wealth of material had been collected about

Johnny Weissmuller and was now available from numerous sources, including many Web sites on the Internet: Weissmuller swimming and Olympic data; Tarzan minibiographies, memorabilia, and fan clubs; *Jungle Jim* fan clubs; Edgar Rice Burroughs bios and fan clubs; and even data concerning my own family history of which I had not been aware. The 1999 Disney animated film *Tarzan* was a smash success, and books and articles about Tarzan were appearing almost monthly, most simply regurgitating erroneous information that had been printed as many as fifty years earlier. We agreed that it was time to tell the true story.

We also agreed that there was a plethora of information on public record—available to anybody who was interested—regarding the Olympic and other national and international swimming records held by Johnny Weissmuller; repeating it here would serve no purpose. And there were certainly far too many clinical, sterile dissections of every film Weissmuller ever made, and antiseptic psychological studies of the Tarzan "mystique," and lists of technical film history and data. It boggled the mind. We decided to forgo that route.

By design, this is not a long book, because it is a simple narrative concerning Tarzan the man rather than a lengthy tome concerning Tarzan the Olympic champion or Tarzan the Ape Man. I have attempted to tell this story in the way that my father told it to me, and to others, spanning many years. His memory was not always good about certain events, and of course he had his own side to tell. My research, and the family documents that I possess, convince me that he was often wrong. So be it. I decided to let Tarzan tell his story in his own way.

To compensate for possible discrepancies in my father's account, I have offered different quoted opinions throughout the text where appropriate. Much of this material (gleaned from people who knew him well, lived with him, worked with him) contradicts the way that Dad remembered his life. Readers may draw their own conclusions.

It would be a mistake to ignore previously published data about my father, or attempt to discredit it all, and start from scratch. Some of that material (such as accounts of his early days in Chicago and the information covering the last tragic years of his life) is pure bunk. Intermixed with that bunk, however, is a lot of fact. Obviously, a weeding process was in order. I have included herein only those stories that my father, over the years, confirmed to me as being authentic—to the best of his memory—or those of which I have personal knowledge from immediate family members, or those that reflect my firsthand experience.

Some of the "behind the scenes" information in this book is painful to remember, let alone write about, but a true understanding of the Tarzan whom I called my "Old Man" can't be found without it. The nickname "Old Man" is not meant to be disparaging. It's what I called him for as long as I can remember, and he's the one who taught it to me—"You listen to what your 'Old Man' says, kid." I just picked up on it, and it became a habit.

If I have made mistakes in this book, I assure you that they are honest mistakes. Nobody living today, with the possible exception of Johnny Weissmuller's fourth wife, Allene, knew my father as well as I knew him. Anything that Dad's fifth wife, María, has ever said about Johnny Weissmuller should be viewed with a jaundiced eye.

This is not a biography of Johnny Weissmuller. There have been too many of those written already. I include biographical material only as a framework for supporting the Weissmuller family story, which is mostly about me and my dad.

—JOHNNY WEISSMULLER JR.

ACKNOWLEDGMENTS

Many people have helped in the preparation of this book or been supportive to me during the years that I have labored over it. I cannot name them all, but recognition is given to Susan Adelle; Susan Allen; Gabriel Azcárraga; Dennis and Diane Blum; Danton Burroughs; Pat and Paul Clisura; Dr. Waldo Concepción; Phyllis Colbert; Cheryl Crane; Roy Disney; Ron Fimrite; Fred Hill; Don Gallery; Marie Windsor Hupp; Chad Johnson; Blake Jones; Allene and Mac McClelland; Mike and Rita Oliver; Carolyn Roos Olsen; Phil Quartuccio; Johnny Sheffield; Maru Eugenia Silva; Owen Smith; Paul and Marilyn Stader; Dr. Stephen Steady; Tisha Sterling; Dr. Bertrand Tuan; Lynn and Tory Winkel; and Jean Hughes Wright.

Special recognition must be given to Jeff Yarbrough and Geoff St. Andrews. Jeff Yarbrough worked with me on a previous attempt to do a book on my father. He interviewed many people on my behalf and worked up a book presentation, but the project came to naught because of my wife's health. We shelved the project. I have taken the liberty of using some of his excellent interview and research material in this book. Thanks, Jeff.

Geoff St. Andrews opened up to us his extensive research on my father dating back more than two decades. He not only provided us with over a thousand special photographs from which to choose, but he also gave us permission to quote from his copyrighted Web site (Johnny Weissmuller: 1904–1984) whatever information we required. Along the way, Geoff also provided us with invaluable editing and research information.

I also wish to acknowledge the support and encouragement of MGM Studios; the Swimming Hall of Fame; *Vanity Fair;* the Motion Picture Home; and, of course, Local 10.

CHAPTER I

Ripples

Family History

Books, magazine articles, newspaper accounts, Internet files and Web site data purporting to be "the true story of Johnny Weissmuller, from birth to death"—I have read them all. Most of them are flawed, and many are pure fiction.

Ambrose Bierce once said that history is "an account mostly false, of events mostly unimportant, which are brought about by [persons] mostly fools." There's a lot of horse sense in that caustic definition, and I suppose that this family history also contains errors as well as information that will be deemed trivial by picky critics. Be that as it may, it is the closest thing to the truth that family records, diligent investigation, and good intentions by this well-meaning fool can make it.

My grandfather, Petrus Weissmuller, met my grandmother, Elizabeth Kersh, in the year 1902, in the small town of Szabadfalu (later renamed Freidorf, meaning "free village" in German), which was

Young Grandpa Petrus with family members.

located in the Banat region of Hungary. He was twenty-five, and she was twenty-two. Petrus was a captain in Franz Josef's Austro-Hungarian Army, and he was on leave with a fellow serviceman who lived in Szabadfalu. Petrus and Elizabeth were introduced following a Sunday church service. The chemistry was there.

Petrus courted Elizabeth by mail and promised to come for her when his enlistment in the army expired. The following year he did so, and they were married in Szabadfalu, in the Catholic church

where they had first met, on the 18th day of April 1903. The newlyweds lived with Elizabeth's parents in the same town.

Szabadfalu and other small towns in the Banat region—such as
Timisoara, Gottlob, Johanisfeld, and Liebling—like most towns in
neighboring Transylvania, had been populated by Germanic settlers
as early as the thirteenth century. As late as 1919, Banat's population
was a mixture of Romanians, Austrians, Serbs, and Hungarians, with
the German-speaking Austrians comprising twenty-three percent of
the total. The Weissmuller clan (originally Weiszmueller, then
Weissmüller—translated as "white miller") were ethnic Austrians.

After boundary changes were made in 1919, following World
War I, the Banat area of Hungary became a part of Romania and
Yugoslavia (bounded on the north by the Marcos River, on the east
by the Transylvanian Alps, on the south by the Danube, and on the
west by the Tisza River). It was at this time that Szabadfalu was
renamed Freidorf. This caused much confusion in later years concerning records of birth. Many people from that region, to this day
(depending upon their birth dates), don't know whether they are
legal citizens of Hungary, Romania, or Yugoslavia. Most Austrians,
however, don't seem to care so much: "Austrians are Austrians!"
they affirm.

On June 2, 1904, Grandmother Elizabeth gave birth to an eleven-
pound boy, whom his parents named Janos (John) Weissmuller. Her
pregnancy had not been terribly difficult, but Elizabeth did complain,
in a letter to her mother, that the baby was "just too heavy." Photo-
copies of the records of the Roman Catholic Parish of Freidorf, Temes
County, Hungary (now Romania), include the following entry:

Baptism Record: Janos (Johann) Weiszmueller, a male, legitimate child, was born 2 June, 1904 and baptized in the parish
church on 5 June 1904. His parents were Petrus Weiszmueller,
a day worker from Varjas, and Ersebert (Elisabetha) Kersch,
of Szabadfalu. The Godparents were Janos Borstner and
Katharina Erbesz.

Ref: Romanian National Archives, Freidorf Parish Records
Baptisms Band 7, No. 40

My grandfather was, apparently, a bluff, hearty man who loved life and people and had grandiose dreams of success and fortune. Mostly, it amounted to just that: dreams. After his marriage, he worked on farms surrounding Szabadfalu, but the work was not steady and generated little income. He began to pressure Elizabeth to emigrate to the United States of America. Elizabeth, who knew that Petrus possessed more imagination than drive, worried that a move to America would change nothing except their location. But Petrus persisted, and, in the fall of 1904, Elizabeth finally agreed. Petrus eventually managed to accumulate enough money to purchase passage for his family on the *S.S. Rotterdam,* which is recorded in official files as having left the City of Rotterdam on January 14, 1905.

While at sea, Elizabeth wrote a letter to her mother, which she sent after arriving in New York:

> I don't know what it will be like there mother. The same for me, I suppose, as it was at home. . . . I'll be busy caring for Petrus and Janos. Maybe I'll work somewhere. Petrus talks of living in Chicago for awhile. He has some cousins somewhere in the city. I hope things will be good for Petrus there. And I hope Janos will have a life that will make his father and me proud.

The manifest of the *S.S. Rotterdam* records the arrival in New York on January 26, 1905, of "Peter Weissmuller, age 27, German race, from Szabadfalu, Hungary. Elisabeth, wife, age 24. Johann, child, age 7/12 [seven months old, out of twelve]. No occupation was given for Peter W., and the family was going directly to Windber, Penn. to brother-in-law Johann Ott. Peter W. was in possession of $13.50 and the condition of health is recorded as good for all three members of the family."

Things didn't work out as Elizabeth had hoped. After a brief visit with friends and family in Chicago, my grandparents moved on to Windber, Pennsylvania, at the urging of other relatives who lived there. There was good money, they assured Petrus, to be made in the coal mines of Windber.

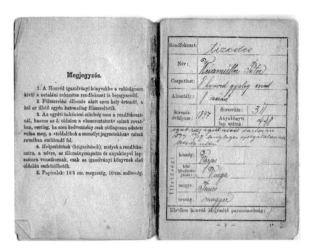

1897 passport of Petrus Weissmuller. Issued just prior to his first visit to the United States.

Grandfather Petrus went to work in the mines, working long, hard hours. By doing so, he defied local folklore; the people of Windber believed that after the stroke of midnight, the ground shifted and demons appeared—demons who could change human intruders into dust. Ignoring this fable, Petrus worked overtime. He needed money. He was determined to return to Chicago and open a beer saloon. He was, after all, a former captain in Franz Joseph's army, and mining was no career for a man of such distinction. In the meantime, Elizabeth gave birth to my uncle and christened him Petrus Weissmuller, after my grandfather. Uncle Pete came into the world in 1905, and he was the first Weissmuller born a United States citizen.

Upon his eventual return to Chicago, Grandfather Petrus, in affiliation with Keely's Brewery Company, opened his beer saloon, and Grandmother Elizabeth took a job as a cook at Chicago's famous Turn-Verein Society. Located in northwest Chicago, the society sponsored many social events; it offered gym classes, had a fencing team as well as a fife-and-drum band, and ran a public playground. Moreover, the society fed just about everybody who attended its events. Elizabeth was a wonderful cook, and in that capacity she

Divorce decree of Elizabeth and Petrus Weissmuller,
Johnny Sr.'s parents.

prospered. She was a respected and valued employee of Turn-Verein for many years.

Petrus, however, went bust after squandering money on friends and strangers alike and, presumably, drinking up large quantities of his stock. Elizabeth paid off his debts after the saloon closed, but by that point the marriage had soured. Petrus resented the fact that his wife was a success and he was a failure. That's when the drunken rages and beatings began.

My father, who almost never talked about those early years in Chicago (other than recalling his swimming experiences), once told me that he used to cover his ears so that he could not hear the screaming and slapping when his father came home drunk and beat his mother. Dad was then only about ten years old, so there was nothing he could do about it, but he sure didn't want to hear it. He began to sneak out of the house at night—sometimes all night—and he often slept underneath the elevated railroad on Cleveland Avenue, covering himself with newspapers. Although he dreaded it, he usually came home in the morning and took the inevitable beatings and cursings from Petrus. Bloodied lips and blackened eyes became almost normal for young Johnny Weissmuller. He once confessed to me that he felt guilty because there were times when he really wanted to kill his father.

He didn't have to. Grandfather Petrus deserted his family in 1916. Grandmother Elizabeth, good Roman Catholic that she was, spread the word that her husband had contracted tuberculosis from working those long shifts in the mines of Windber. The "demons," she swore, had finally tracked him down, and he died a horrible, hacking death of the black lung disease around 1918. I suppose she wasn't up to the tribulations of a Catholic divorce, and this seemed a simple way for her to lay her husband to rest; or perhaps she simply made up the story of his dismal demise to make herself feel better.

Her story was so widely believed that it persists in most "biographies" written about the Weissmuller family to this day. But it simply is not true. I have in my possession the divorce decree of Elizabeth and Petrus, dated February 20, 1925. It reads, in part,

> ... subsequent to their intermarriage the Defendant [Peter Weissmuller] has been guilty of extreme and repeated cruelty toward the complainant [Elizabeth Weissmuller] without any provocation or just cause thereof; particularly in the month of February A.D. 1924 when said defendant while using vile language struck the complainant a blow in the face [numerous other accounts of bodily harm are listed and, finally,] ... again on the 20th day of November A.D. 1924 when said defendant threatened to kill said complainant. ...

The divorce was granted, of course, and it is rumored that the old reprobate lived to a ripe old age, remarrying along the way and spawning a large brood of little Weissmullers. However, nobody, including close family members, really knows what happened to Grandfather Petrus.

Elizabeth took complete charge of the Weissmuller family of Chicago after 1916, but Petrus still came around and hassled her often. I am not sure when he finally died, but he was not grieved by the rest of the family.

The story of my grandfather is a tragic one, but no different from the thousands of other emigrant stories that record dreams, disappointments, and despairs. We praise the successes of those who came to settle in America and try to forget the failures. Sadly, Grandfather Petrus was a failure, and he plays no further part in this story.

CHAPTER 2

Waves

Road to the Olympiads

My father was once quoted as saying, "Before swimming, there was nothing . . . only surviving." I never heard him utter those words, but he did tell me that his only intimate contact with water before he was eight years old was during the horrible experience of the Saturday-night bath in a big, old, porcelain bathtub. Then, one wonderful day, Grandmother Elizabeth bought him a pair of water wings and nudged him into Lake Michigan off Fullerton Beach in Lincoln Park. Dad said to me, "I can't really explain it except to say that it was like coming home. I had found my element. Swimming? Hell, for me it was easier to learn than walking."

I have read in various "Weissmuller biographies" that Grandmother Elizabeth took my father to the beach at the advice of her family doctor, who told her, "swimming may be the only thing that can save your sickly son from an early grave!" I once mentioned this to Dad, and he said, "That's a load of crap! Skinny? Yeah. Sickly? Never in my life!"

Still, it's possible that swimming did save my father from a life of juvenile delinquency and perhaps even prison. He was, by his own admission, a wild one in his youth, and he hung out with an even wilder crowd.

What started out as a series of childish pranks, such as snatching ice-cream cones from little old ladies on the street, progressed to heavier infractions: snapping cables off streetcars, placing Bull Durham tobacco cans filled with explosive potash and sulphur on streetcar tracks on the 4th of July, and, eventually, some rather serious street-gang fights. People got hurt. Some members of my father's gang moved on to snatching purses and rolling drunks. My father and a few of the others objected to that, and the gang split into factions. Inevitably, they began to fight among themselves.

As my father told his original biographer, Narda Onyx, and later repeated to me in a somewhat modified form,

> I found myself backed into a corner by six punks who decided to teach me a lesson. I had been working out as a boxer in the local gym and fancied myself a tough guy, but this was a tall order. Still, I was winning the match until a local Irish street cop broke up the brawl. He gave me a pat on the head and praised me. The Catholic priest at Saint Michael's Parochial School gave me a pat on the butt and ordered me into the chapel, where I spent hours on my knees and said dozens of "Hail Marys." After that, I only confessed very minor sins!

Dad said even that didn't help much. He had so many cracks across his fingers with the sharp edge of a ruler, and so many kneeling sessions in the chapel, that one day, after being forgotten for hours by an avenging priest, he "passed out." He told me that he had faked the entire scene, but it was so convincing that Grandmother Elizabeth angrily took him, and his brother Pete, out of Saint Michael's and enrolled them in Menier Public School, a mixed tutoring place for boys and girls alike. Dad was twelve, and he was still more fascinated with boxing and swimming than with girls, and he said that he wished he could have maintained that kneeling posture.

My father went through some rough times during his childhood, but he also experienced many happy times. He went to the opera often with Grandmother Elizabeth, and, while listening to the tenors, he decided that it really wasn't such a bad thing to have a high-pitched voice (at an early age, he'd injured his vocal chords by accidentally impaling his throat while trying to jump a picket fence in emulation of his movie hero Douglas Fairbanks).

In fact, young Johnny saw a way to make money out of this vocal impairment. He struck a deal with the neighborhood vegetable peddler, who was getting old and hoarse from shouting out his daily sales pitch: if he could yell out "Tomatoes! Potatoes! Fresh beans and cabbages!" in a loud enough tenor voice to attract the attention of local housewives, the peddler would pay him with baskets of fruits and vegetables. It worked out just fine. Grandmother Elizabeth was especially happy. She was desperate for money; in addition to working at Turn-Verein, she cleaned floors or did anything that helped support her family. As she saw it, her son's new job sure beat blowing up streetcar tracks, and it helped immensely with her household budget.

As I said, Dad did not often talk about this time of his life, but from time to time he did reminisce, and a few stories slipped out. "I'll never forget the visits to your grandmother's relatives who owned a farm somewhere in the country outside Chicago," he once recalled. "They had cows and pigs and chickens and turkeys and goats and all kinds of other animals we seldom saw in Chicago. These relatives, like almost all of their neighbors, were Germans and Austrians, and they held this thing they called a 'Schlacht,' where they roasted a pig, played God-awful music, danced, drank gallons of beer, had potato-sack races and yodeling contests. That's where I perfected my yodel, by the way."

I said, "Dad, I read somewhere that the sound experts in the film studio took your yodel and reworked it and put a lot of other sounds in there to make the Tarzan yell."

He answered, "Well, yeah, they did that at first, but then I just practiced it and learned how to imitate it. Like this. . . ."

I cringed.

How much of the on-screen Tarzan yodel was really Dad's voice and how much was the sound mixing of Hollywood technicians we

A young Johnny, far right, with lifeguard friends.

will probably never know, but I do know that he could perform one
hell of a Tarzan yodel with his own pipes, especially after he'd had
a few drinks. I've never heard anyone else come close—nor, I'm
sure, has anyone in Acapulco.

A lot of the information that I have concerning my father's
growing-up period in Chicago came from Grandmother Elizabeth.
She told me that Grandfather Petrus had been a bookie on the side,
in his bar, and that her two boys eventually got into a little book
themselves. For Dad, that didn't last long. He abandoned the bookie
caper and took up swimming so enthusiastically that he had little
time left for anything else. Uncle Pete, however, was lured by the
excitement of it all and sank deeper and deeper into this shady
lifestyle until it finally consumed him. It wasn't that he was a bad
guy—he was just seduced by the fast buck. He was also seduced
by a few fast women, which led to a bout with syphilis in his late
teens. My father took time off from his regimented athletic training
schedule to take care of Pete. The brothers exchanged harsh words

over that. Good health and hard work were almost gospel to Johnny Weissmuller.

Dad dropped out of public school at about the age of twelve. He worked as a bellhop and later as an elevator operator to help with family expenses, and he attended swimming school in his spare time. In 1916, he made the YMCA swim team. A short time later, he met the man who would change his life forever—the man who would set him on the track to swimming and Olympic stardom.

"A Stopwatch Doesn't Lie!"

The story about how my father met "Big Bill" Bachrach, the head coach of the Illinois Athletic Club of Chicago, has been told in so many versions that the truth may never be known. I never got around to asking Dad about it. A *New York Times* account, published some time afterwards, is probably closest to the truth:

> A little more than a year ago, a member entered the Michigan Avenue home of the Illinois Athletic Club with a slender 16-year-old youth who had ambitions to become affiliated with the Chicago Organization which was famous for its record-breaking swimming teams. The boy knew that he could swim. He had read about the tricolor swimmers, Perry McGillivray, Norman Ross, Hebner, Vosburgh and others and he wanted to cast his lot with them. The member, however, was skeptical of the youngster's chances of gaining a place amongst the galaxy of stars already in the I.A.C. fold. But after listening to the kid's appeal for more than a month, he finally promised to introduce him to coach Bachrach, the premier trainer of watermen.
>
> Finally, one day, the boy's persistence was rewarded and he was taken over to the I.A.C. pool and brought before coach Bachrach. "Here's a fellow who thinks he can swim," was the member's half-hearted explanation for taking up the coach's valuable time with an unknown. . . . Slipping into the pool, the skinny youngster traveled through the water with a crude stroke but one that showed unusual power. Immediately

Bachrach knew that he had what is known in the sporting parlance as a "find."

In a later interview, Bachrach explained that the "find," Johnny Weissmuller, "held his head so high out of the water, and kicked and splashed so that he reminded me of a dog swimming. I don't think I've ever seen worse form in my life. But I held a stopwatch on him, and a stopwatch doesn't lie! The kid finished the run in just under record time—and he wasn't even trying!"

Personally, I think that what made my father such a great swimmer was that same awkward, crude, head-held-high style that Bachrach commented on. Dad developed it on his own. Most swimmers either rotate their heads from side to side, taking gulps of air with each revolution, or they keep their faces down in the water for thirty or forty seconds at a time and then switch to alternating sides to gulp air. These two forms of swimming are somewhat similar to the way a low, squat motorboat moves through the water—pretty to watch but with a hell of a lot of water drag on the submerged hull—as opposed to a hydrofoil, which planes upward and lifts the hull out of the water, reducing drag. I think Dad probably developed this head-elevated style because he swam in dirty waters as a child and wanted to keep floating debris out of his mouth.

If you watch the Tarzan movies in which he acted, you will better understand what I am trying to describe. That was his natural stroke. Bachrach—or Bach, as some people called him—didn't try to change this style, because he realized early on what was happening. Instead, he developed it and improved upon it, teaching his new pupil what was to become the famous Weissmuller "six-beat-double-Trudgen crawl stroke," which Bill Libby described in a *Saga* magazine article published in January 1965: "He swam with his back arched and his head, shoulders and chest thrust out of the water. He shook his head loosely from side to side, inhaling and exhaling on both sides. He cocked his elbows high, drove his arms down into the water hard and behind him hard. While he kicked six beats to every cycle of his arms, he considered kicking of consequence only to maintain balance, stay high in the water and reduce drag."

It was an Englishman, by the way—J. Trudgen—who first demonstrated the overhand-double-arm stroke in 1893, and an Australian named Richard Cavill added the scissor leg kick in 1900.

His training under Bachrach officially began in October 1920, when my father was sixteen. Bach pushed him hard, first working on the arms and on push-and-pull exercises while Dad's feet were trapped inside a floating inner tube, then concentrating on leg action. Later came breath-control instruction and, most importantly, trying to teach this excited young pup to relax. Dad often jumped the gun while awaiting the starter's pistol: "Relax," Bachrach said to him over and over, "and when you see the guys to your left and right start to dive, follow them, but dive shallow, as you have been trained to do, then stay high and keep high. Within a few seconds, you won't see the other swimmers, because you'll be ahead of them. Relax! Relax! Relax!"

And, of course, the help that Dad got from his teammates and fellow championship swimmers was also invaluable: he learned Norman Ross's rolling, relaxed, arm-and-body stroke, as well as his starting technique; Perry McGillivray and Harry Hebner worked with him on end-of-the-lane turns. In the end, he adopted the best of all these styles and melded them into Olympic gold.

Finally, Bachrach's star pupil was ready. Bach entered him in a tryout race in the junior men's one-hundred-yard event in 1921. He lost! Dad didn't like to talk about it—I once pressed him about it, and he grumbled, "The damned bathing cap slipped down over my eyes, and I lost time at the turn trying to get it clear. Yeah, I lost, but it was only an unofficial race. I never lost an official race in my life! Never!"

And I never brought up that subject again . . . *ever*.

Competition

Later the same year, my father won his first two official races: the National AAU (Amateur Athletic Union) fifty-yard event at the Duluth Boat Club; and the one-hundred-yard event, where he competed against Stubby Kruger at Brighton Beach, New York, finishing in record time. He was soon being called by newspaper sports reporters such names as "Flying Fish," "Human Hydroplane," and "King of Swimmers."

In 1922, for a national championship event sponsored by the Shriners, Bachrach took his swim team to Honolulu, Hawaii. Dad was scheduled to race against the "invincible" Duke Kahanamoku (Duke and his brother, Samuel, were at the time considered to be the two fastest swimmers in the world).

"The Duke refused to come to the States [mainland] to race me," Dad recalled, "so it was decided that I would go to Hawaii to race him. Some said it was because the Duke thought he really couldn't beat me, but I think he just wanted to race me on his own turf."

Dad said that to prepare for that race, he swam across the Pacific Ocean while still aboard the boat that was carrying him to Hawaii. Seeing my eyebrows rise at that one, he laughed and explained. Coach Bachrach persuaded the crew to rig up a swimming pool in number-two hold (the second aft of the bow, and usually the largest deck). Essentially, they reversed the tarp covering the hold, tacked it back down again, and half filled it with water. Bach then threw in a half-inflated inner tube tied to a rope and watched as his prize pupil swam in place for some seven hours each day preparing for the event. But the Weissmuller-Kahanamoku contest never happened. The Duke backed out of the race at the last minute. He had developed a sudden "illness." However, on this trip to Hawaii Bachrach's team broke thirteen world records, with "the Flying Fish" collecting most of the trophies.

Harry B. Smith, in a *Chicago Chronicle* article that appeared shortly thereafter, wrote,

> Johnny Weissmuller, world's champion swimmer and holder of all records, outdoors and indoors, from 50 to 100 yards, is a most bashful youngster for a Chicago-raised lad and one who has seen as much of the world as he has.
>
> Johnny, fresh from his recent Honolulu trip, where he smashed more records than anyone can conveniently remember, came to the *Chronicle* offices yesterday by appointment for photographs and an interview.

Johnny Weissmuller at the Illinois Athletic Club, 1923.

The photographic part of it was run through nicely.

But when it came to interviewing Johnny, finding out all his likes and dislikes, it was a good thing that William Bachrach, swimming coach of the Illinois A.C. and mentor in extraordinary to Weissmuller was . . . a member of the party.

As for Johnny, he simply slumped into a chair, hid himself behind a fresh copy of *The Sporting Green,* and replied, if at all, in monosyllables.

"Yes," said the expansive Mr. Bachrach, "Johnny loves the women. He just dotes on them. Haven't you got any women reporters around here that Johnny can talk to while we are having this interview? You see, Johnny is looking for a wife. But she must possess certain qualifications: Must have money! Must be a good dancer and love hot dogs and ice cream! In addition, if she's good looking, it will not do any harm!"

That got a rise out of Weissmuller. "Aw go on . . . quit your kidding. What do I want to get married for?"

The swim star is only 18 years of age, having celebrated

that birthday while in Honolulu. He's a big chap so far as size goes, but weighs no more than 175 pounds.

Bachrach [said that this was] Johnny's greatest asset. "He has the strength of former champions, but without their weight to pack around in the water . . . but he eats too much. He thinks there's nothing but meat and ice cream in the world. I try to get him to eat more vegetables and the like, but it's hard work. Still, he's young and full of life and does so much swimming that he doesn't need to worry. Four or five years from now he will have to pay more attention to his diet. . . ."

Legerdemain

During the remainder of 1922 and throughout 1923, my father won race after race. He was obviously in great shape, but there were other worries. The big event was still ahead: the Olympiad of 1924, scheduled to be held in Paris, France. That posed a serious problem. In order to qualify for the American Olympic team at the final tryouts in Indianapolis, Indiana, in June 1924, contestants were required to prove U.S. citizenship by presenting a valid birth certificate. Dad had no such document.

Complicating things even further, stories speculating about his birthplace made national headlines. The *New York Times* reported that Illinois Representative Henry Riggs Rathbone had publicly expressed doubts as to Johnny Weissmuller's citizenship. Questioned about this by reporters, Grandmother Elizabeth stated for the record that her son "was born in Chicago, will be 20 years of age next June, and has no intention of being anything but an American citizen." The next day the *Chicago Tribune* ran the headline "Can't Bar Weissmuller from Olympiad: Was Born Here!"

In response to the *Tribune's* embrace of the Weissmullers' assertion, Representative Rathbone softened his stance somewhat by saying, "He may very well have been born in Chicago. It's just that there's no record of his birth in the city, and he and his family have produced no evidence to support their claim."

But as the Paris games drew nearer, Olympic officials told Dad that he needed to produce legal proof of his citizenship (his mother's

Preparing to take a dive.

sworn statement was not enough) in order to obtain an American passport. My father and Grandmother Elizabeth (with the full concurrence and connivance of Uncle Pete) then hatched a plot to switch his official birthplace from Chicago to Windber, Pennsylvania.

Back then, in the baptismal records of Windber's St. John Cantius Catholic Church, there was an entry for my father's younger brother, Petrus. Today, that entry records the baptism of my father. "Petrus Weissmuller" is written in one hand, but "John" has been inserted between "Petrus" and "Weissmuller" in a distinctly different ink and penmanship. Church officials, to this day, aren't sure when or how the record was altered.

The brothers, in order to solidify the deception, switched names and birth certificates: Peter, though always called Pete, claimed from the late 1920s until his death in 1966 that his "real" name was John Peter Weissmuller and that he was a Romanian born in 1904. My father alleged from 1924 onward that his true name was Peter John Weissmuller and that he was born in Pennsylvania in 1905. I have in my possession Uncle Peter's certificate of U.S. citizenship, which lists his former nationality as Romanian. Peter, of course, was born a U.S. citizen in Windber in 1905, but—having switched birthplaces with my father in 1924—*he* became the foreigner and, of necessity, the "older" brother.

Presented with my father's falsified records, Olympic and government officials were finally satisfied as to his bona fides. He was allowed to participate in the final Olympic tryouts. The athletes chosen during that event (including "American citizen" Johnny Weissmuller) sailed for France aboard the *S.S. America*.

Olympics and Fame

In the 1924 Olympiad, my father won gold medals for the one-hundred-meter freestyle (beating out both the Duke and Samuel Kahanamoku—who came in second and third, respectively); the four-hundred-meter freestyle (beating out Arne Borg of Sweden and Andrew "Boy" Charlton, the sixteen-year-old Australian sensation—who came in second and third, respectively); and accepted a third gold medal as team anchorman for the eight-hundred-meter men's relay. The president of the French republic also presented a special medal to my father in recognition of his incomparable performance.

Dad was very happy and very proud, but he was also very nervous. Thoughts about the possible results of the scam that he and his mother had perpetrated haunted him his entire adult life. He worried that they would take away his medals, prohibit him from ever competing in the Olympics again, publicly disgrace him, and possibly destroy his personal and professional lives. All of this, however, he viewed as secondary to what a scandal might do to Grandmother Elizabeth. She had been so proud, and, should the deception become known, it would surely devastate her, especially since the world would certainly blame her for it. Dad decided to take the secret with him to his grave. And that's exactly what he did. No one—including his five wives, his three children, dozens of relatives, thousands of friends, or millions of fans—ever knew the full truth of the matter.

Upon his return to the United States, Johnny Weissmuller found himself to be a celebrity. He was even invited to the White House to receive congratulations from President Calvin Coolidge and Chief Justice William Howard Taft. Hungarian? Romanian? Austrian? Hell, as long as he kept quiet about it, what did it matter? He was an American hero!

My father told me that he was invited to visit rich and famous people all over the United States, but Coach Bachrach did not approve of this socializing nonsense at all. He said, "Johnny, you're in training. Forget 1924, that's history. We've got to think about 1928."

Bachrach vetoed most of my father's invitations. He did, however, approve a 1926 invitation from Douglas Fairbanks to visit him on the set at MGM Studios in Hollywood, where he was working on a film called *The Black Pirate*. Fairbanks was one of Bachrach's heroes too.

My father said that what he remembered most about that meeting was being introduced to a guy who looked much older than he did in his films, seated in a barber's chair and having his chest shaved. This wasn't exactly what he had expected, and Dad raised an eyebrow. Mr. Fairbanks chuckled and said, "If you ever get into movies, Johnny, be sure to shave every bit of hair from your body. It looks dirty on screen. In fact, it is dirty, and smelly, and probably not even hygienic." Dad told me that he wasn't sure what "hygienic" meant, but he grinned and nodded his agreement.

Over lunch, Dad was introduced to a man named Sol Lesser, who totally ignored him. Lesser was pushing Fairbanks to look at a film project based on Edgar Rice Burroughs's *Tarzan of the Jungle*. Fairbanks wasn't buying it: "I don't really think so, Sol; it's just not my cup of tea." Then Fairbanks glanced at my father and said, "How about this lad? His name is Johnny Weissmuller, he's a national swimming idol, and he even looks like Tarzan, don't you think?"

Dad said that at this point Lesser turned and really looked at him for the first time. "Afraid not," Lesser replied. "What we need for this role is a star!" Subject closed.

Six years later, MGM begged my father to sign a contract to play the lead in *Tarzan the Ape Man*. He refused.

For the remainder of 1924, and from 1925 to 1928, my father continued to set world record after world record in AAU national freestyle swimming competitions. In 1925 alone, he set three world records and nine American records. He continued to be hailed as "the best swimmer in the world."

Coach Bachrach had always discouraged Dad from swimming in events longer than five hundred meters, telling him that he was a sprint swimmer, not a long-distance swimmer. In 1926, Bachrach finally relented and permitted him to enter the three-mile Chicago River Marathon. Dad had pressured Bachrach to agree to this because he wanted to beat the record held by Richard Howell of the Chicago Athletic Association. Howell had declined to enter the event that year, but Dad was sure that he could beat his record of the previous year. He almost pulled it off, but he encountered unusually strong winds and waves. Although he did win the competition, his time of fifty-six minutes and forty-eight seconds fell twenty-eight seconds short of Howell's record.

In January of 1927, the Illinois Athletic Club sponsored an invitational swimming meet in which my father swam the one-hundred-yard freestyle race in an incredible 49.8 seconds, setting a new American record. Still, Coach Bachrach never let up on his swimming star; he entered him in a host of events, and Dad won them all. Hands down. Then, at last, it was time for the 1928 Olympics.

My father collected two more gold medals for the U.S. team, which were presented to him by Queen Wilhelmina of Holland. "After presenting me with the gold medals," Dad recalled, "Queen Wilhelmina said, 'Just a minute, young man,' and she held me by the hand as she presented to me her personal medal. She said, 'You

must be proud, Johnny. You have done your country a great honor.'
I was awed, but all I remember thinking was 'She looks just like my
mother!'"

Immediately following the 1928 Olympics, my father was awarded
his second presidential citation, participated in a ticker-tape parade
down New York City's Fifth Avenue, was presented with the keys
to the city by Mayor Jimmy Smith, and received yet another medal,
this one presented by New York's Governor Smith. He didn't have
time to use the keys to play around, as he'd wanted to, because
Coach Bachrach took him shortly thereafter to Japan to compete
against Japanese swimmers.

Dad told me that luckily, a few days before the event was to take
place, Bach learned that the Japanese trained in cold water, and they
planned to increase their chances of winning by filling the pool for
the match with extremely cold water. Bach scotched that by forcing
Dad to sit in a tub filled with ice water until he grew accustomed to
it. He won every event.

The Japanese swimming coaches were so impressed with this
new young swimming sensation that they offered him the job of
helping to train their students for the next Olympiad. He turned
them down, and they told him that he would be sorry. (As it turned
out, the Japanese team swept the 1932 Olympic swimming events,
for they were trained to endure anything—even the coldest of water.)
Dad laughed and said, "We'll see, but don't hold your breath. My
friend Buster Crabbe will also be swimming in those events, and
I'm putting my money on him!"

My father told me that story, I believe, sometime during the
1950s when I was living with him (and Allene, his fourth wife, and
my second "mom") in their Los Angeles home. He explained that
in the four-hundred-meter race, Jean Taris of France was the odds-
on favorite, Takashi Yokoyama of Japan was billed as number two,
and Buster Crabbe was not thought to have a chance. "Hey!" he
added, "I've got a clipping of that here somewhere." Dad bustled
over to his desk and returned with his scrapbook. "Here, read this!"
One paragraph said it all:

Johnny shakes hands with Katsuo Takaishi at the 1932 Olympiad.

One of a trio of swift Japanese swimmers, Takashi Yokoyama, lowered the Olympic record to 4:51.4 in qualifying rounds, still well off Taris's world mark of 4:47. But the Japanese challengers were never threats in the final, where Taris went to the front and held a two-length lead at 200 meters. Crabbe closed the gap with 100 meters to go and caught Taris halfway through the final stretch. The 10,000 fans—including 1924 400-freestyle champion Johnny Weissmuller—jumped to their feet, yelling loudly for Crabbe to get the gold. Weissmuller even climbed a fence to get closer for a better look. As Crabbe touched the wall, he looked up and saw Taris's head bob, a sure sign the Frenchman had just come in No. 2. Crabbe was the gold-medallist in 4:48.4 to Taris's 4:48.5. Crabbe commented later that that one-tenth of a second changed his life. Paramount Pictures offered him a $200-a-week movie contract. . . .

Dad said that he and Buster Crabbe had never really been close friends because they were both so damned competitive. Later on, Crabbe acted with Dad in a less-than-memorable film called *Swamp Fire,* and he even played the role of Tarzan in a couple of films, but those roles were also less than memorable.

"However," said Dad, "after that Olympic win we became buddies. Well—sort of."

Change of Pace

My father retired from competitive swimming in 1929, and, by his own admission, he became a beach bum, giving exhibitions and lessons in swank Florida hotels in exchange for room and board. He also teamed up with three other Olympic athletes—Helen Meany, Martha Norelius, and Pete Desjardins, as well as the Clown Prince of Diving, Stubby Kruger—and he worked on a highly profitable filmette, *Crystal Champions,* produced by Grantland Rice. In their off-hours, Dad and Stubby Kruger went out on wild romps through town, once setting off a battery of fire alarms. "Stubby and I went to a Miami jail over that one," Dad told me. "It took a lot of high-powered string pulling by Steve Hannigan and other film promoters to get us out."

Shortly after getting out of the Miami jail, Dad secured, through Bachrach, a well-paying contract with BVD (Bradley, Voorhies, and Day) swimwear. His days as a beach bum were over. Dad said that Bachrach came down, sometime in 1929, for what Dad thought was a social visit, and then he dropped the bombshell. Bachrach approached Dad as he was climbing out of the pool after a practice session, waited until he had toweled off, handed him a piece of paper, and said, "Sign this."

Of course, Dad signed it. He always did everything that Bachrach asked of him. But he was curious. "When I asked Big Bill what I had signed, he said, 'Johnny, you've just become a pro! This is a contract with BVD swimwear for five hundred dollars a week. You'll act as a representative of their product and travel the country giving swim shows, appearing on talk shows, signing autographs, and handing out literature promoting their products. You've got it made, my boy!'"

Dad was dumbfounded. Five hundred dollars a week? That was a fortune in those days.

He replied, "My God, Coach, what can I say?"

Bachrach said, "Say good-bye, you big ox, and get the hell out of here!"

While recalling this parting, Dad said, "There were tears in Big Bill's eyes. There were tears in my eyes. But, as always, I did exactly what my coach asked me to do. I was happy, but also sad. The realization that my days as an amateur athlete had just ended hit me hard."

Dad loved William Bachrach. I think this man became for him a substitute for the father who had never really accepted him as a son.

All that my father ever really wanted was to be an athlete. Swimming was his life, and he had dreams of starting a swim school when he got too old to compete. In one of our conversations, he said,

I remember a time back in 1927 when I was training for the annual Chicago Three-Mile Marathon in Lake Michigan. My brother, Pete—who tried but never quite made it as a swimmer—was alongside me in a rowboat marking my progress, when a violent storm hit with almost no warning at all. The double-decker excursion boat called *The Favorite* flipped over a few hundred yards from us and sank immediately, with maybe fifty or sixty people aboard. She settled on the shallow bottom, right side up, and by the time Pete and I reached her, all I could see was the ship's captain, seated in a chair with a smoking cigarette still in his mouth, holding on to the hand of a little boy. The captain was in shock, and he kept mumbling, "My God! My God! There are people down there, and I can't swim!"

Dad and Pete both dived and started bringing up passengers as fast as they could. They managed to pull up about twenty, and of those twenty, most were children; nine died. Dad continued,

Those poor little kids never had a chance, because they didn't know how to swim. What a damned useless waste! I said to myself, "I'm going to teach kids how to swim!" And I had the chance to do so years later, after I stopped competitive swimming and went to work for BVD. Hell, I was making five hundred dollars a week, and with a few years' savings from that kind of money I could have easily started a world-class swimming school—which is all I ever really wanted to do. Instead, I got greedy and went for the big bucks. Biggest damned mistake of my life.

Dad, who had consumed a few drinks during the telling of this story, got up from his easy chair, walked to his desk, and returned with a small cedar chest, from which he removed a faded envelope. He wiped a tear from his eye and said, "To the day that I die, I will never part with this letter, which I received from a woman in 1962. Here, read it."

Jack Dempsey, left, and Johnny pose in their BVDs.

The letter read as follows:

Dear Mr. Weissmuller,

I have seven children, and one day my seven children will have their young ones. The circle of life will continue forever or as long as God grants this earth to remain fertile with the atmosphere. But only you, Mr. Weissmuller, are responsible for this vast miracle that has come to touch my life, because it was you who rescued me from certain death, and enabled me to marry and have my children. I shall always impress upon the minds of my young ones to say a prayer of thanks on your behalf and, God willing, these prayers will last through a part of eternity. . . .

In 1930, my father wrote a short autobiographical book for the Houghton Mifflin Company with Clarence A. Bush titled *Swimming the American Crawl*. He dedicated the book to "William Bachrach, my coach, and to the members of the Illinois Athletic Club." In the postscript, he wrote, "Anyhow, I've certainly had a great time swimming, and if I had my boyhood days to live over again, I can't imagine anything more interesting to do than just what I have done."

Dad worked for BVD for perhaps two years, and he never could have imagined himself making so much money. He almost lost it all, however, by making a brief appearance in a Paramount film called *Glorifying the American Girl*, starring Mary Eaton. John Harkrider (Florenz Ziegfeld's theatrical designer) talked him into doing it. His was a short scene about great lovers, starting with Adam and Eve. Dad played Adam, and he and Mary were clothed only in fig leaves. When BVD found out about it, all hell broke loose. "Johnny Weissmuller in a fig-leaf swimsuit does not promote our product!" company officials proclaimed.

They threatened legal action against Paramount and suspension of Dad's contract. It was all finally worked out when the studio took my father's name out of the credit line and agreed to show him only in one long-distance shot. That was Johnny Weissmuller's introduction to filmmaking.

CHAPTER 3

Whitecaps

Bobbe Arnst and Hollywood

When I finally got to the age where I was considering matrimony, I visited my father in his home, and we had a man-to-man talk about it. I asked him to tell me about his first marriage. He said,

Well, I guess you might say that the time was right. Maybe overdue. I'd been swimming and training for so many years that I really didn't have time for girls in my life, and that just wasn't natural for a kid my age. I'd had a couple of affairs of the heart—one with a girl named Lorelei, in Chicago, who deserted me and married another guy, and one with a girl named Helen, who was a member of the U.S. Olympic team in Amsterdam. She didn't desert me, she just forgot about me. I had just about had it with women. But, again, I was lonely.

In February 1931, I accepted an invitation from Pete Desjardins to meet a girl named Bobbe Arnst, who was at the time singing with Ted Lewis's band at a club in Miami. She was blonde and pretty. Even if she'd been ugly, I might still have

Bobbe Arnst, Johnny's first wife.

fallen in love. I needed a woman, and not just a one-night stand. I needed a woman who wanted me, a woman who would love me and take care of me, a woman to call my own. We were introduced that night, went swimming the next day, and were married by a justice of the peace in Fort Lauderdale two weeks later.

Bobbe gave up her singing job and accompanied Dad on his road travels, promoting the BVD line. On a trip to Florida, at the Biltmore Hotel in Coral Gables, Dad spent a lot of time in the hotel pool, where he met a sad-looking little boy, befriended him, and taught him how to swim. While the boy appeared to be lonely, he was never alone. Two big guys in flashy suits always accompanied him. Dad was intrigued but asked no questions. This went on for some time, Dad patiently holding the kid's body up in the water while showing him how to kick properly. All the while the two mysterious body-guards looked on. Then one day the little boy was gone, never to return.

Shortly thereafter dad received a package, delivered to his hotel room, that contained a magnificent gold watch, something like a solid-gold Rolex. The enclosed note read,

Thanks for taking care of my son.
—Al Capone.

The newlyweds finally wound up in Los Angeles and rented a small flat in the Leyenda Apartment Hotel on Whitely Avenue. The first thing Dad did, of course, was skip down to the Hollywood Athletic Club on Sunset Boulevard for a swim.

"And that swim," said my father, "led to my introduction to Hollywood."

Newsreel of the Newsstands, Carol Benton (1932):
WANTED: NUDE ACTOR.

DIRECTOR HUNTS FOR WEEKS FOR HE-MAN WHO CAN ACT WITHOUT CLOTHES: . . . For six weeks, Director [Woodbridge] (Africa) Van Dyke searched for a hero for his new picture, *Tarzan*, and took tests of practically every actor in Hollywood without finding the man he wanted. . . . "The hero of my picture has to look naked, not undressed," said Van Dyke. "Most actors without their clothes look as though they [are] just about to step into the bathtub. The college boys I tested looked fine—until they stripped. Then they were ill at ease, embarrassed. 'Tarzan,' brought up in the jungle, would be utterly unconscious of his lack of clothing. But I couldn't find an actor in Hollywood who wasn't dependent on his clothes!"

It was then that somebody thought of Johnny Weissmuller.

"He has spent most of his life in bathing trunks, so he doesn't notice the lack of clothes," said Van Dyke. "Johnny is built the way men were meant to look. I felt that he was my 'Tarzan' as soon as I saw him in a pair of pants and a sweater, and when I saw him without them—my search was over!"

Of the many actors and athletes that Van Dyke had earlier tested, he said: "Charles Bickford isn't young enough, Johnny Mack Brown isn't tall enough, Clark Gable has no body, Tom Tyler is the best so far, but he's not muscular enough. I want someone like Jack Dempsey, only younger."

"Woody" Van Dyke found what he was looking for in Johnny Weissmuller.

That's how the press of that era described Johnny Weissmuller's introduction to Hollywood, but my father always told a somewhat different story. According to him, he was "discovered" by Cyril Hume, the screenwriter. Hume also worked out at the Hollywood Athletic Club, and, seeing my father swim one day, he introduced himself and offered him a chance to test for Metro Goldwyn Mayer Studios. Dad didn't know what the hell he was talking about, so he asked, "Test for what? I've already got a good job. I don't need to test for anything!"

Hume explained that he had just been assigned to write a screenplay based on the Edgar Rice Burroughs character Tarzan. Dad replied, "So . . . what's that got to do with me?"

"I'm offering you a chance to work in moving pictures, Mr. Weissmuller."

"Yeah? Do I get to meet Jean Harlow?"

"Piece of cake."

The next day, Hume took his discovery to lunch at the studio commissary, and Dad did meet Jean Harlow—as well as Joan Crawford, Norma Shearer, Clark Gable, Wallace Beery, Marie

Dressler, Jackie Cooper, and even Greta Garbo. The Old Man was hooked.

Then Hume took Dad to an on-lot executive bungalow to meet Bernard Hyman, the producer of the Tarzan film, and Woody Van Dyke, the film's director. Johnny Weissmuller's movie career almost ended right then and there. Hyman asked him to take off his shirt so they could see his muscles. When Dad was down to his shorts, both Hyman and Van Dyke punched and pinched him for a while, and then Hyman asked him what his name was. When Dad told him, Hyman said, "Weissmuller? Well, we can't have that. Much too long for a marquee. Never mind. We can come up with something shorter."

By this time, Hume could see that Dad was boiling, so he started laying it on thick: "Mr. Hyman, don't you know who this is? This is Johnny Weissmuller, the swimming champion of the world! The man is famous! You can't change his name!" Hyman replied that he had never seen the name "Weissmuller" in *Variety*, so the kid couldn't be all that important.

Hume suggested that they authorize a screen test, and Van Dyke said that he didn't think it was necessary: "This is the guy I want for the Tarzan role. He looks the part, and he doesn't really have to act much, anyway. He just has to follow orders."

After Hyman and Van Dyke had bickered with each other for a few minutes, they came back and offered Dad a seven-year optional contract at a starting salary of $175 per week. He politely declined. They were shocked and asked Dad why he wasn't interested. He told them that BVD was already paying him five hundred per week without six-month option periods, and he had three more years on that contract. He wasn't sure that he was cut out to be an actor, and he thought he'd be better off sticking with the sure thing. Then, after a bit more wrangling, he simply walked out.

I guess nobody had ever turned MGM down before, because suddenly Johnny Weissmuller was a hot property. The word was out: "Get him back! Get Weissmuller!"

It wasn't easy. The people at BVD flatly refused to terminate my father's contract, and then they and MGM got into it hot and heavy.

It was finally settled when the two parties agreed that if BVD would release Weissmuller then MGM would permit all of its stars to be photographed in BVD swimwear, including Garbo, Crawford, Harlow, and even Marie Dressler. My father was then called to the MGM front office to sign a contract for seven years at a starting salary of $250 per week, with built-in raises upping it to more than two thousand dollars per week.

Dad was about to affix his signature to the contract when one of the executives said, "Oh, there is one minor condition that you should be aware of."

"Yeah, what's that?"

"You have to get rid of your wife."

"What the hell are you talking about? Get rid of my wife? Does that mean kill her or divorce her? Forget it! I'm not about to 'get rid of my wife,' not for you or anybody else!"

They didn't believe him. They had been playing this fish for weeks now, and they decided it was time to set the hook firmly. Dad recalled them saying, "Well, take it or leave it. We can't have a hot male property in the Tarzan role who is known to be a married man. It just won't work. Take it or leave it!" To their surprise, Dad again threw up his hands in disgust and walked out.

The following day, he was called back to the office, where he signed the contract. Still married. But it didn't end there, of course. The studio continued to work not only on Dad but also on Bobbe: "Do you want to stand in the way of Johnny's career? Look, you're a singer. You have a profession, and we can help you in that profession. And, as a bonus, we'll even throw in ten thousand dollars to help you get started again. What do you say? Let him go."

My father went on to make *Tarzan the Ape Man,* and in April of 1932 he went to New York for the premiere, leaving Bobbe in Hollywood. By the time he returned, she was looking at divorce as a reasonable option. After all, she was a former Ziegfeld girl and a singing star in her own right. She wouldn't have any trouble getting a well-paying job, and MGM would help her, and with ten thousand dollars as seed money....

Dad recalled her saying, "I'll go visit mother . . . and I've still got a voice, and . . . ten thousand dollars is a lot of money, Johnny." My father said he just shook his head and replied, "Yeah, I guess you're right, Bobbe," ashamed of himself as he said it. By June, divorce proceedings were under way.

Shortly thereafter, Bobbe Arnst commented in an interview, "Hollywood took my Johnny from me. It wasn't his fault any more than it was my own. They wanted him, and they got him. . . ."

"Don't You Remember?"

Johnny Weissmuller's next "official" wife was the Mexican Bombshell, Lupe Vélez. Three more were to follow, but I think it's important to mention that Dad had more than his advertised five marriages. Maybe they were common-law marriages, but I know for a fact that he lived with more than five women in a husband-wife relationship.

I first discovered this back in 1957 or 1958, while I was acting in a film called *Andy Hardy Comes Home*. I arrived at the lot at about 7:30 in the morning, and I heard a woman screeching. I looked around and saw her running down the outside steps of a nearby building. Her face was rouged, and even though it must have been about seventy-five degrees, she was wearing a full-length mink coat. Running up to me, she threw her arms around my neck and began sobbing, "Oh, my son! My son!"

I said, "Lady, who are you?"

She replied, "I'm Legs Lanier! I'm your mother, of course. Don't you remember? I was married to your father. You're my son!"

I was flabbergasted, but I soon got the lady quieted down and learned that she was Toni "Legs" Lanier—like Bobbe Arnst, a former Ziegfeld girl—who had recently been married to Eddie Mannix, who ran MGM Studios. However, she swore to me that she had once been married to Johnny Weissmuller. I knew that MGM had paid off Bobbe Arnst to divorce Dad, but I'm not sure to this day what happened in the case of Legs. In those days, marriages between movie-studio employees sprouted and then disappeared as if by magic—often with all official records mysteriously removed.

I finally extricated myself from this tangle of arms and legs and walked away in a daze. This woman must have been quite beautiful at one time, but the wear and tear now showed, and she was obviously crazy. "Don't you remember?"

Hell, if she was "married" to my father, it had to have been between his marriages to Bobbe and Lupe, and my father hadn't even met my real mother at that point. I was still to be born! So how had she recognized me? Then I realized that my father and I looked remarkably alike as young men—except for the fact that he was six-foot-four and I am six-foot-six. Legs must have seen a vision of her former "husband" walking through the studio lot.

Woody Van Dyke, the director of *Tarzan the Ape Man,* had a reputation for being an ogre on the set. Although Dad had not liked the man when they first met in Bernard Hyman's office, he came to appreciate his abilities as a director. He said, "Woody was tough, but fair, and he really knew how to handle action shots. I had learned all about discipline and how to follow the rules from Bachrach, so I had little problem getting along with Woody. We never became buddies, but we worked together well as long as I did what he asked of me. That was easy. I got along with just about everybody at that time."

Tarzan the Ape Man, with Maureen O'Sullivan as "Jane Parker," was a smash hit: the movie ranked among the top ten box-office hits of 1932, along with *Grand Hotel, Shanghai Express,* and *Dr. Jekyll and Mr. Hyde.* The combination of Johnny Weissmuller and Maureen O'Sullivan was absolute screen magic. "Me Tarzan. You Jane" suddenly became an expression known around the world. Laughing about this one day, Dad said,

You know, I never actually said, "Me Tarzan. You Jane." It was really just two words: "Tarzan. Jane." Over the years, so many people got it wrong that I just gave up and let them have it their way. Humphrey Bogart once said to me, "Kid, I never

Poster for Tarzan the Ape Man, *Johnny's first Tarzan movie.*

said 'Play it again, Sam,' either, so don't feel bad." But that just goes to show you how little people really know about me. My first really important words on screen were misquoted!

Perhaps, but *Tarzan the Ape Man* was one hell of a kickoff for a movie career that spanned sixteen years and included twelve Tarzan films. But not everybody was enthusiastic about Tarzan's debut. A Chicago newspaper quoted Elizabeth Weissmuller, who was unhappy that her son was billed as "Miami's own Johnny":

> He's Chicago's own Johnny. . . . But then I suppose that's what they'll call him when his picture opens here. It's rather hard to keep up with the movie business, and I haven't really decided what I do think about Johnny as an actor. Of course, I haven't seen him yet, but, you know, now he'll be in Hollywood most of the time, and ever since he did go out there I've been worrying about him and his food and his clothes.
>
> Mothers are a little funny about such things. I suppose they're all alike and think of their children as never growing up, but really sometimes I even had to tie Johnny's tie, but Bobbe Arnst, his wife, is a sweet little girl and she takes care of him all right. . . . He's a good-looking boy . . . he's nicely built and his swimming has made him graceful, but that doesn't make him a good actor. . . .

Stalag Hollywood

The next two Tarzan films, *Tarzan and His Mate* and *Tarzan Escapes,* were also big box-office hits. All three, however, were tainted with public and studio controversy. As I said earlier, my father played twelve Tarzan roles from 1932 to 1948; Maureen O'Sullivan was his Jane from 1932 to 1942. It almost didn't happen that way, because Maureen, after her second or third Tarzan film, made up her mind to quit playing Jane. In an interview published years later, she explained:

> Between the violent reactions of an Anglo-Saxon puritanic public because of what they termed my "nude" scenes in the

The young Tarzan with Maureen O'Sullivan as Jane.

first couple of Tarzan films, and the equally intolerant reaction of MGM executives, who then clothed me in virgin-white swim costumes which looked like they came off the rack at Macy's, I was thoroughly disgusted with the whole scene. I actually had friends who called and offered me sanctuary in their homes, or cabins in the mountains, where I could hide in my shame.

The fact that Olympic gold medallist Josephine McKim performed the "nude" scenes, as my stand-in, and the fact that only her bottom really showed in the underwater swimming shots, made no difference. I was a promiscuous harlot in the eyes of many of the viewing public. It even went so far that rumors spread that Johnny Weissmuller and I were lovers in real life. That was not true. There was only one man in my life, and that was John Farrow [John Villiers Farrow, a motion picture director and writer]. I later married John and bore him seven children, including Mia [Farrow]. Johnny and I were great friends, nothing more.

Thalberg [Irving Thalberg, head of production at MGM] and Mayer [Louis B. Mayer, studio chief] were behind most of this harassment. I disliked both men intensely and finally decided that I had had enough. I later changed my mind when things cooled down a bit. I'm actually glad that I did, but I still have a sour taste in my mouth about the studio system in those early days. They were really nothing more than tyrants who controlled every aspect of the lives of their employees. And, star or not, you were nothing more than that to them; simply an employee, to be used and discarded at will.

Certainly, "moral censorship" in those days was completely out of control. In fact, it became silly. According to critic Molly Haskell, the "most ludicrous image was not Tarzan and Jane in their Cole of California jungle wraparounds, but Cheeta and his simian siblings in body stockings trying to meet the Production Code requirement that exposure of the sex organs, male or female, child or animal, real or stuffed, was forbidden."

Slave Labor—Metro Goldwyn Mayer Studios

My father made only six Tarzan films for MGM before switching over to RKO Studios. He said that all of the studios were slave drivers, but undoubtedly the worst of the lot was MGM. Dad and I talked about this often, especially after I started acting myself, but one of the best descriptions that I have ever heard of what it was like to work for MGM is in a taped interview that William Reed, coauthor of this book, once played for me.

Bill made the tape, circa 1978, with film director John Huston while they were collaborating on Huston's autobiography. In an early portion of the tape, Huston said about film studios in general,

> Control you? Hell, they owned you! You couldn't even get married without studio approval. . . . If some infraction of the rules was observed on the set, no matter how minor, it was reported to the front office. You never knew who reported it, but reported it would be. The spy system was very professional indeed. The studios went to extraordinary lengths to keep their houses in order. . . . Some bad things went on in that studio world . . . sometimes you felt like you were in a prison . . . but you must remember that we went along with it. Call it greed, call it self-preservation, call it whatever you want, but we went along with it.
>
> We went along with it because we had sold our souls for money. My starting salary as a screenplay writer for Warner's was five hundred dollars a week, and when they took up my option it went to $750 a week. Do you realize how much $750 a week was in the 1930s? Hell, schoolteachers were lucky to get fifty dollars a week in those days. Moreover, don't forget that even though the studios punished you for the slightest infraction, they also took care of you, professionally and personally. Drunk driving? Public brawling? Possibly even murder? If *anything* jeopardized the career of important studio employees, especially stars in whom the studio had invested millions, it was somehow covered up. Power? Yeah, sort of like the early Rockefellers, Morgans, and Carnegies. Police chiefs, mayors, even governors jumped to do their bidding. Politics and power: that was the name of the game.
>
> After *We Were Strangers* . . . I think around 1948 . . . anyway, before I made *The African Queen* . . . I had some financial setbacks and found myself deeply in debt. Paul Kohner, my business manager, arranged for me a loan of $150,000 from MGM as part of a two-picture contract with them. This was my first experience with Metro, and I must say I was impressed. Glamour, glamour, glamour. Luxury, luxury, luxury . . . but

underneath it all control, control, control. They kept their troops in line. And the troops ran the gamut from the Marx Brothers to Greta Garbo.

It was all controlled by L.B. Mayer. Irving Thalberg had almost toppled Mayer. Thalberg was a boy genius. He didn't act like other producers, because he never wanted his name to appear on the screen. He liked to control from behind the scenes, and he was so good at it that he began to threaten the rule of Mayer. Mayer solved that by sending Thalberg on a trip to Europe. When young Irving returned, he found himself as just another producer. L.B. had taken over completely. So the prince was retired, and the king took over. No matter; little changed. Both men were consummate bastards. I went on to make *The Asphalt Jungle*, where Marilyn Monroe got her start in films, and *The Red Badge of Courage* for Metro, but that was about all I could take of that Mickey Mouse farm.

My father always said pretty much the same thing:

Thalberg once actually said to me, "We discovered you. We made you what you are. Play by our rules, or don't play!"

Mayer vetoed any idea of my taking acting lessons. "We don't want him to act, we want him in action," he said. They thought that my voice was too high-pitched, so they increased the underwater sequences, wrestling matches with jungle cats, dives from rocky cliffs, and endless scenes of me swinging from vines.

I remember seeing a handwritten note on a revised script for the 1936 *Tarzan Escapes* script that read "Mr. M. objects to the [increased] dialogue scenes. He doesn't want dialogue, he wants more stunts for Johnny."

Richard Thorpe, who directed four of Dad's Tarzan movies, said, "Mayer wanted more shots of Tarzan's face and body than he did of Jane's. He once said to me, 'Make him look like Valentino . . . and do whatever you want with her.'"

Edgar Rice Burroughs was quite upset with Hollywood. He didn't like the way that they were handling his Tarzan material. In excerpts from interviews commencing sometime in the mid-1930s, he said,

> A man whom I described as coming from a family of nobility, son of Lord and Lady Greystoke, who was eventually sent back to England, educated, and was multilingual, now speaks on film in nothing but grunts and monosyllables. . . . Scenes that depict black men killing white men—which certainly happened many times—are, by Hollywood standards, grounds for firing directors. . . . Nudity in any form is taboo. No nudity in the jungle? Where are these people coming from? Have they never had any experience with real life? . . . Cheeta and Boy sleeping together, but Jane sleeping alone in her own room—like some kind of a nun room mother? I never wrote any fiction like that! I can't imagine anybody who would—except perhaps a Hollywood screenwriter.

My father was also angry at Hollywood. He did not like the simplistic dialogue that he was given to work with—such as "Umgawa!"; "Tarzan eat now!"; "Tarzan swim now!"; "Cheeta come!"; "White man bad!"; "Tarzan break guns!"; "Talk twist Tarzan's tongue!"—and the fact that he was actually discouraged from trying to act. This frustration was part and parcel, of course, of the wrong-side-of-the-tracks syndrome that he struggled his entire life to overcome. He wanted to cross over those tracks, but he was prevented from doing so, first by Hollywood, and later by the fact that he was just too well established in the minds of the public as Tarzan the Ape Man. He said, "At first, I thought all this mumbo jumbo was funny. After I saw it on film a few times too many, I began to resent it."

But this feeling of resentment didn't arise until later. When Dad first started working on the Tarzan films, he was only twenty-seven, and he loved rubbing elbows with famous people and diving off rocks and wrestling with alligators and lions and riding on elephants and playing with Cheeta. "I loved it all," he said. "I was having the time of my life—especially with the animals!"

And naturally he was also pleased that he was making a considerable amount of money on the side from product endorsements. In 1933, for example, Wheaties launched its "Breakfast of Champions" campaign, and the first endorsements for that breakfast cereal came from Johnny "Tarzan" Weissmuller and baseball great Lou Gehrig.

Cheeta

During the 1960s and '70s, my father occasionally visited me in San Francisco, where I was working as a longshoreman and also doing some acting in films and on the stage. On one of those visits, the conversation turned to the animals that he had worked with over the years. He said that there had been so many that he could scarcely remember them all, but one of his all-time favorites was Cheeta the chimp.

> The grooming and greasing up and costuming in a silly loincloth that barely concealed my putz was bad enough, but the biggest problem I faced was learning how to handle the wild animals. Cheeta was my first experience in that department. When I first met him, I put out my hand, and he tried to bite it. I thought, "Either he doesn't like me, or he's trying to establish who is the boss here."
>
> I decided it was the latter, and the next time he tried that I pulled out my knife, which had a big brass knob on the handle, and tapped him smartly on the noggin. He shrieked and jumped back and ran around in circles, made as if to attack me, then apparently thought better of that and sat down and huffed and puffed for a few minutes. When I saw that he was quieted, I held out my hand, palm up, and Cheeta shuffled over, sideways, and took my hand. After that, we were friends. I think that friendship was firmly cemented after I once saved his furry little butt from drowning!

As Dad remembered it, they were shooting some scenes in a pond near the Santa Anita racetrack. He was rowing a canoe to the other side of the pond, and Cheeta was perched near the bow. When they came close to shore, Cheeta mistook the green algae near the bank for solid ground. The next thing Dad knew, the chimp's head was a couple of feet under water, and his hairy arms were desperately reaching for the sky. A few seconds later, Cheeta sank completely, and the only sign left of him was a big air bubble. Dad pulled the canoe alongside the bubble, reached down, grabbed the chimp by the scruff of his neck, and pulled him into the boat. He said that fifty pounds of monkey clung to him like a wet rag for the next hour and a half, and from that day on Cheeta and "Tarzan" were inseparable.

There were many chimpanzees named Cheeta during the sixteen years of Tarzan films, but there was really only one as far as Dad was concerned, and that was his "swimming buddy." After "aquatic" Cheeta retired to the Los Angeles Zoo, my father often went to visit him. He said that when Cheeta died it was almost like losing a son.

Chimpanzees are certainly not friendly with just anyone. For example, they don't like foreigners—by that I mean people who don't speak the kind of language they are used to hearing. Cheeta once jumped up, ran across an outdoor picnic table, and punched an English gentleman—who was relating a joke in an idiom that nobody present could really understand—in the nose so hard that it bled. The gentleman sat there quietly for a moment and then said, "My word, that was very uncivilized behavior!"

Other Costars

"And then," said Dad, "there was Jackie the lion. Jackie was the biggest cat that I had ever seen in captivity. When I first met him, his trainer was holding him closely on a leash. I reached out to pet him, and the trainer said, 'Be careful! He doesn't know you yet.' I said, 'Sure he knows me. We already talked about that.' The trainer looked at me as if I was out of my mind and actually jumped back as I grabbed Jackie by the mane and gave his head a vigorous shake." Dad said that Jackie then "grinned and began licking my arm with his raspy tongue. From then on, he slobbered all over me every time we met, and I had to hold him off. His sandpaper tongue not only licked off most of my makeup but also scratched the hell out of my skin."

One of the most difficult tasks, Dad insisted, was teaching a lion what to do when the director said "Cut!" Lions simply have no understanding of that word, which can be a problem when you're in the middle of an intense "wrestling" match. These wrestling scenes were typically shot with male lions, as they have manes, which give them a more ferocious look than females. Dad explained that male lions also

> have a tendency to slap you a little harder than you slap them, and they don't know when to stop. Fortunately, our lion trainer knew just how to handle the situation. Unfortunately, the trick was just a tad embarrassing. It required rolling underneath the beast, reaching up with the tips of your toes, and tickling his family jewels. This, of course, relaxes the lion and makes it easier to get him disengaged. Provided he doesn't fall in love with you.

"The crocs," Dad assured me, were the hardest to ride,

> because they thrashed around something awful, and their scaly hides ripped my legs up. I rode and "killed" a lot of crocs over the years, stabbing them with my fake knife. The blade slid up into the hilt, and "blood" spurted out with each stab. We never hurt the animals, of course, but sometimes I wanted to. I remember one day a croc broke the tape around his jaws and chased me around the outside of a water tank. I almost didn't make it to safety. You might be able to outswim a croc, but you can't outrun one!

I said, "Dad, you've told me that so many times I can't keep count. Okay, I promise I'll never try to outrun a crocodile, but I doubt that I'll ever get the chance. As far as I know, the only crocs

Tarzan on set, riding an elephant who sports rubber ears.

in California are in the zoo!" He smiled knowingly and said, "Well, the next time you go to the zoo just remember one thing: you can't outrun a croc!"

Dad always had cuts and abrasions from riding animals, and elephants were no exception. He said that they were very scratchy, so the animal handlers used blowtorches to remove the bristly hair from their backs, but it was still like riding a wire brush. "We always used Indian elephants," Dad said, "which are more easily domesticated than African elephants, and we had to be careful not to grab their ears, which were made of rubber and then glued on. The Indian elephants have smaller ears than the African variety, so we had to make them look African, you see."

"Tarzan's" favorite elephant was called Emma. She was a sucker for apples and peanuts, and he taught her all sorts of tricks, even how to lift him up with her trunk at a signaled command. Speaking about the same Emma in a documentary film produced by London Weekend Television in 1997 and titled *In Search of Tarzan*, Maureen O'Sullivan said, "Most of the animal trainers were very good, but Emma's trainer was a cruel man. He often jabbed her with a sharp stick on the soft underside of her trunk when she missed a cue or failed to obey his commands exactly. Having endured this kind of treatment patiently all day, Emma waited until the shooting was over, then walked over to her trainer, picked him up with her trunk, threw him on the ground, and stomped him." Maureen did not appear to be too upset about this.

As I said earlier, Dad was a bit miffed with the Hollywood gibberish he was compelled to utter on screen, but aside from that he was having a ball as Tarzan of the Apes. He was making a lot of money and spending it with abandon. He had a new car, all the girlfriends any man could desire, and plenty of free time in which to entertain them. He said, "I sure as hell didn't have to stay up nights memorizing my lines for the following day. And without having to do more than mumble jumble, swim, and play with animals, I made three very successful films by the time I was only thirty years of age. What more could a man ask for?"

CHAPTER 4

Breakers

Lupe Villalobos Vélez

Lupe Vélez, nicknamed by the public "Whoopee Lupe," "the Mexican Wildcat," and even "the Mad Vélez," was born Guadalupe Villalobos Vélez in San Luis Potosí, Mexico. Some contemporary accounts state that she was of peasant stock, but that is not true. She came from a distinguished family.

Lupe was educated in a Mexico City convent and later in San Antonio, Texas. Her wealthy and influential parents moved her around from school to school because she didn't last long in any institution due to her volatile temper. She was all but uncontrollable. She eventually rejected schooling entirely and set out on her own. Lupe went from a musical stage revue in Mexico City, to a part in Richard Bennet's *The Dove* in Hollywood, to *The Music Box Review,* to parts in a series of Hal Roach comedies, to the role of a wild mountain girl in the Douglas Fairbanks production *The Gaucho.* That last role led to stardom. Lupe Vélez was hot stuff, and she knew it. Unfortunately, my father did not.

Although Lupe, 109 pounds of well-proportioned curves, stood all of five feet tall, she liked big men. Recovering from the breakup

Lupe Velez, Johnny's second wife and a star in her own right.

of her long-term relationship with Gary Cooper, she was in the market for another big guy when she spotted "Tarzan" getting into an elevator in the same New York hotel in which she was staying. They had both just returned from the grand premiere showing of *Tarzan the Ape Man*. Lupe's eyes measured Tarzan's chest and broad shoulders, and she nodded approvingly.

Dad said that soon after he'd settled himself in his room the phone rang. He picked it up and heard a soft Latin voice purr, "*Hola, Meester Tarzan, I am Lupe Vélez. My room ees just below yours. Would you like to have a dreenk with me?*" Dad replied, "Yeah, sure, and I'm John Barrymore. I'm also tired and going to bed!" He laughed as he remembered the moment.

> Would you believe I actually hung up on her? Well, thirty seconds later the phone rang again, and I was treated to a torrent of Spanish that I couldn't understand but had no problem interpreting. Somebody was very pissed! Then, after a distinct slam, the phone went dead. I called the front desk and asked if Lupe Vélez was staying at the hotel. The desk clerk informed me that she was, and I asked him to connect me to her room.
>
> "I'm sorry," I said. "I thought you were a crank. Invitation still open?" It was, and I walked right into the most dangerous lion cage that I have ever entered in my life!

I think my father really loved Lupe Vélez. She was good for him: she made him laugh. She was also bad for him: she drove him crazy. Dad just couldn't handle her. In his comparative innocence, he was in no way equipped mentally or emotionally to handle this worldly wise, Mexican spitfire. I don't think anyone could have handled her. She was a manic depressive who swung from delightful highs to oppressive lows. From an enchanting pixie, she could turn into an avenging *bruja* in the blink of an eye. Her affair with "Tarzan" was an on-and-off thing. After their return to Hollywood and their separate film careers, Lupe broke off with Dad and took up, briefly, with Errol Flynn. Then she broke off with Flynn and resumed her affair with Dad because, as she explained it to a newspaper reporter, "I like beeg guys! John-ee, my Pop-ee, ees a beeeg guy!"

The story of how Johnny Weissmuller and Lupe Vélez were married at the instigation of Jackie the lion is apocryphal, but my father always liked it and, I suspect, embellished it from time to time. Still, when I questioned the story's authenticity, he stuck to his guns, and this is the way he told it to me:

It was a Friday night, and I was leaving the set when I discovered that Jackie had been left unattended on an empty stage by his trainer. I suspected that the guy was around the corner getting drunk—again. I got tired of waiting and decided to take Jackie home with me. I took him by the leash and led him to my car. Jackie was delighted with the entirely new experience, and he settled into the front seat of my convertible as if he had been doing this all his life.

We almost had a few collisions along the way with astonished motorists, and a drunk at a stoplight who leaned over to ask me directions to Venice almost had a heart attack when Jackie leaned out and belched in his face. I waited for him to ask me directions to the nearest AA clinic, but he burned rubber a fraction of a second before the light turned green. Miraculously, Jackie and I finally made it home.

We had no sooner settled in than Lupe showed up unexpectedly. Jackie greeted her at the door. She patted him on the head and said, "¡Hola, amigo! ¿Cómo estás?" Shedding her gloves, she continued in rapid Spanish, "Johnny, ya es tiempo de casarnos. Pero no quiero ningún maldito león en mis casas. ¿Comprendes?"

Even before she translated this tirade for me, I got the message. She would marry me, but Jackie was definitely out! I assured her that I understood perfectly, and a few weeks later I drove to Nevada, where Lupe was working on a film, and we were married by a justice of the peace. I left Jackie at home, of course.

After we were married, I moved in with Lupe at her two-story, Spanish-style mansion on Rodeo Drive in Beverly Hills, and I thought I would be happy with her forever. She was the funniest person I'd ever met, and I really believed she loved me, but it didn't take me long to figure out that our different lifestyles were going to be our first marital problem: I was a day person; she was a night person. She loved parties; I hated parties. She drank constantly; I didn't drink at all. She smoked constantly; I didn't smoke at all. I loved the water; she hated the water. I tried everything I could think of to make her happy, and I went along with her constant-party routine as long as I could, but I was not at all pleased with the way things were turning out.

Dad bought a thirty-four-foot schooner and changed its name from *Chula* to *Santa Guadalupe*, in honor of Lupe. He then planned a trip to Catalina Island to celebrate, but Lupe got so sick that they had to turn back. Later, Dad bought another boat—a sixty-foot sailing vessel named *Allure*. That worked a little better, but it was apparent to all concerned that Lupe was just not a water person. Period.

It occurs to me that perhaps Lupe's aversion to water was aggravated by the fact that Dad spent a good portion of his time aboard boats. Almost every weekend, he raced his *Allure* to Catalina Island against Humphrey Bogart in his *Santana* and Errol Flynn in his *Sirocco*. All three would bet on the outcome. On one of these excursions, after they had anchored at Catalina, Dad went aboard *The Sirocco* to collect money from Flynn, who had lost the race. Errol was drunk and belligerent. *The Sirocco* had a small, old-fashioned cannon mounted on her bow—the kind that had a fuse at the touchhole—and Flynn pointed this cannon at Dad's boat, took the cigar from his mouth, and lit the fuse, muttering, "I'll sink you, you sumbitch!"

Dad ran over and kicked the muzzle upwards (it was actually a tiny thing, mounted on a swivel, so he's lucky he didn't break his foot), and the two men stood there in awe as the cannonball shot straight up in the air and then descended vertically. It missed them by a scant few feet and dropped cleanly through the upper deck of *The Sirocco*. After a few seconds, Flynn burst into uproarious laughter. The cannonball was not the explosive kind, and the boat was rafted up, so there was no danger of her sinking, but even so it could have been a disaster. Lupe did not think it funny at all, and it resulted in another knock-down, drag-out fight between her and Dad.

Dad, Bogie, Flynn, Raoul Walsh, and their other sailing cronies had quite a reputation as hell-raisers in those days. Lupe must have had her hands full. The sailing and the racing were actually just excuses for partying. A black man called the Duke was the skipper of Dad's *Allure*, and he liked to party as much as the rest of them. After docking, the Duke would sometimes join the unholy crew for drinks on the fantail. Then it was time for cocktails at the yacht club. Blacks were not allowed in, so they solved that problem by swearing, jointly, to the club manager that the Duke was a "Blue Hawaiian." For Lupe, I am sure, this constant routine of practical (and often dangerous) jokes was almost as unpleasant as sailing and the seasickness it caused her.

Lupe hated boats in general, but the ones she hated most were the powerboats. And the worst of that lot, Dad said, was John Wayne's *Wild Goose*. She was a converted U.S. Navy AVR (Aviation Rescue Craft) with three English Allison engines that were so damned noisy that before Wayne fired them up to charge his batteries, he had to send the Duke up and down the Gold Coast to warn people. The resulting noise was almost window-shattering. Lupe absolutely hated it. The frequent sailing excursions on the *Allure* were bad enough, in her mind, but at least that boat had a sail, and there were occasional periods of peace and quiet. She refused to go near *The Wild Goose*.

When I was young, I, too, occasionally went with Dad aboard *The Wild Goose*, and I agree with Lupe: that boat was not only noisy, but she was also crazy. She had an antiaircraft "ack-ack" station located aft, which had been converted into a giant poker table, and this somehow descended from a dome. Any cabinet you

Johnny Sr. on the deck of his boat, the Allure.

opened was more than likely to be stocked with booze, and you got the feeling that you were in a Las Vegas casino rather than aboard a yacht. Think of your wildest dream, and you'd probably find it somewhere on *The Wild Goose*. Damnedest thing I've ever seen.

Wayne used to race *The Wild Goose* against Gene Autry's vessel, a converted PT boat called *PT Joe*, and he always lost. Gene's boat was very fast. With the exception of Autry, who was not really one of the "guys," most members of this wild group hung out in exclusive Newport Beach haunts such as Art LaShelle's Christian's Hut or the Balboa Bay Club; they were also regular visitors to Catalina Island and Acapulco. Their escapades are legends. They once put a boat on a truck and "sailed" it from Newport to Las Vegas. They also put a train (I think it was a small locomotive) on a barge and towed it to Santa Catalina Island. And they got away with it. The police, the Coast Guard, the public all loved it. Things were a bit more relaxed back then.

I have good memories of Dad's sailing days with the "wild bunch"; my wife, Diane, and I were married aboard Humphrey Bogart's *Santana*. But in their heyday, those guys were beyond crazy. For sure they drove Lupe crazy, and marital rumbles became more and more frequent.

Dad said that when he'd finally had enough of the constant bickering, he began to cast about for solutions:

> I persuaded Mother to quit her job at Turn-Verein and come live in California near us. I thought her influence might help to tame Lupe down a bit. Forget it. Mother was unhappy about the move, and Lupe was totally indifferent to what Mother did, or did not, think of her continuing public escapades. And we fought constantly. Boy, did we ever fight! Neighbors began to complain, and reporters began to hint at trouble in "Tarzan's Tree House," stuff like that. I was at my wit's end.

In a newspaper interview published around this time, Lupe had this to say: "Do you expect John-ee and I to sprout ze leetle weengs and fly like angels? . . . Of course, John-ee and I disagree a leetle. But it is only like other peoples . . . just the small arguments! We, what you call, squabble a leetle. . . . I am vairy tired. . . . We are going back to Hollywood to rest. I was so seeek we had to cancel a personal appearance in Boston. I have not had wan rest in ten years—not even wan leetle vacation!"

Dad told me that Lupe could speak good, unaccented English when she wanted to, but he qualified that by saying that she never lost her Spanish accent completely. She knew that her accentuation of the Spanish-Latin idiom was good publicity. She only used the "Pop-ee" kind of thing for interviews or public appearances. It was considered "charming" by her fans, and they expected it of her. Today, I'm sure, that kind of reporting would be considered racist mimicry, but in those days it went unchallenged.

My father told me that, increasingly, he and Lupe were separated for long periods of time. She was constantly traveling, doing talk shows and film shoots all over the world; and he stayed in California, worked at the studio, and took care of an obnoxious parrot and two Chihuahua dogs, Mr. Kelly and Mrs. Murphy. Dad didn't much like the parrot, because the bird kept calling him "Gary." Lupe had purchased the parrot when she was still living with Gary Cooper. For obvious reasons, Dad disliked the bird, but he absolutely hated the dogs. I don't think I've ever heard him speak harshly about any other animal. Lupe, of course, adored her pets.

In self-defense, Dad rescued a big mutt named Otto from the city pound. Standing on his hind legs, Otto was as tall as Dad himself. Lupe, naturally, detested Otto, fearing that he might harm her two little darling dogs, but she accepted him—barely—after seeing him lying contentedly on the floor with Mrs. Murphy asleep on his back and Mr. Kelly chewing on his tail.

Dad and Lupe called a truce, but it didn't last long. The fights became more frequent, and Lupe started talking about maintaining two separate households. Then she was off to London to work on another project. Dad had a few weeks of downtime before his next

Tarzan film, so he decided to join Lupe there and see if they could work things out.

"Next Time around, Johnny!"

This was one of my father's favorite stories. I must have heard him tell it at least forty times, and it always changed somewhat—according to his audience or how much he'd had to drink—but this is the version that I like best:

Lupe was staying at the Claridge Hotel, probably London's most exclusive and conservative establishment, and she had booked a marvelous suite. When I arrived, it was all love and kisses. Great! After an hour or so of marital bliss, Lupe fell asleep, and I picked up a book and lay back with a contented smile on my face.

The next thing I knew, Lupe jumped out of bed, grabbed one of her shoes off the floor, and began pounding me on the head, all the while screaming and cursing in Spanish. From what I could make out, she was accusing me of having affairs with other women while she was traveling and working and trying her best to save our happy marriage. I simply could not believe this was happening!

I leaped out of bed and tried to grab her and calm her down. She ran out of the room, into the hallway, screaming at the top of her lungs, "¡Socorro! Help mee! Murrder!" I was wearing only my pajama top and was naked as a jaybird from the waist down, but I ran down the hall hoping to catch her and try to stop this uproar. Suddenly, to my right, a door opened, and a matronly lady in nightcap and gown stared at me in wonder. I nodded, mumbled an apology of some sort, and continued the chase. On the second turn around the corridor, the matronly lady shouted at me, "Faster, Johnny! You'll catch her the next time around, I'm sure!"

I did catch her the next time around, and she was as tame as a kitten. It was as if nothing at all out of the ordinary had happened. We spent the rest of the night in peace, but the following morning an eviction notice was quietly slipped under the door. We had half an hour to pack and leave the premises. Lupe read the note and started giggling. I read the note and also started to giggle. Soon we were both laughing hysterically, tears running down our cheeks. Then we started packing. We were interrupted by a knock at the door. I opened it, and a red-faced hotel manager apologized for the eviction notice and asked us to please stay. I was confused: "Stay? Why this sudden change of heart?"

The manager coughed and then whispered, "It seems, sir, that last night you passed the door of Queen Wilhelmina of the Netherlands, and she spoke with you. She informs me that she once presented you with two gold medals following the Olympic games, as well as one of her own. It appears that she has a great fondness for you, and she quite firmly stated that if you leave she is leaving also. I do apologize again, sir, and I hope that you will do us the honor of remaining."

After Lupe and Dad returned to California from London, my father left almost immediately for Florida to start work on *Tarzan Finds a Son!*, in which Johnny Sheffield would play "Boy." Lupe went back to Europe, and soon her name began to appear in the newspapers; there were stories of her affairs with other men. When she returned home, Dad joined her briefly during a filming break and saw that she was sporting a diamond tiara worth a small fortune. He questioned her about it, and she assured him that it was a mere "trinket" and said she had paid for it herself. Tarzan may have been a primitive by Lupe's standards, but even Tarzan knew that his wife could not afford a trinket like that on her salary. It was the beginning of the end. Dad returned to Florida in a foul mood.

The end came suddenly and violently. Dad completed work on the film and went home to California. Lupe informed him that a "stranger" had entered the house and poisoned Otto. He was dead. Mr. Kelly and Mrs. Murphy now had the run of the house, and the parrot squawked his approval. My father was crushed. He'd really loved that dog. "In fact," he told me, "I think I loved that dog more than I loved my wife—at least at that time." It was a sobering realization.

Dad called Lupe a lying bitch and accused her of killing his dog, and she finally admitted it. By this time, Mr. Kelly and Mrs. Murphy were barking and nipping at Dad's feet, and the parrot was screaming, "Gary, Gary, Gary!" Instead of hitting Lupe, Big John walked over to the parrot, grabbed him in his huge fist, broke his neck, and threw him at Lupe's feet, muttering, "Goodbye, Gary."

Of course, that was the end of the marriage. My father packed his bags and left. He never again returned to the house on Rodeo Drive. A short while later, Lupe Vélez issued a statement to the press: "Marriage? Eeet steenks!"

Dad didn't talk of Lupe often—I think the memories were just too depressing. But once, at a party where he was discussing his wife's escapades with some close friends, I did overhear him relate a funny story about Lupe. Dad said that on more than one occasion while they were still married, he had to go next door to Gary Cooper's house and "persuade" Lupe to come home. He said that he usually wound up carrying her under his arm while she shrieked and scratched like a wildcat.

Tarzan Finds a Son!

Although my father was very upset about the sad ending of his marriage to Lupe, he was enthusiastic about the prelude to that disaster, which was the film *Tarzan Finds a Son!*, and he told me many times in later years how very special this movie was to him. He was delighted with Johnny Sheffield, who played Boy, and Johnny Sheffield was delighted to meet and work with Johnny Weissmuller. Some of Sheffield's comments about working with my father are included in an interview he did for *Matt's Bomba Movie Guide*. I talked and corresponded with Sheffield recently, and he told me to use whatever material from that interview I found useful; he also sent me an updated version with additional comments. Johnny Sheffield recalls,

tttttt ttttttttttttttttttttttttttttttttttttttttttttttttttttttttttttttttttttttttttttttttttttttttttttttttt

Johnny Sr. with Maureen O'Sullivan, Cheeta, and Johnny Sheffield in Tarzan's New York Adventure.

I can only say that working with Big John was one of the highlights of my life. He was a Star (with a capital "S"), and he gave off a special light and some of that light got into me. Knowing and being with Johnny Weissmuller during my formative years had a lasting influence on my life. I didn't know it then, but as time has passed, I see very clearly how Big John was different from most and how being around him started a clock ticking in my head a lot like the one in his. Here was a champion, an undefeated Olympic world champion. He was never defeated during his [official] swimming career! [And to me] the most important thing was that Johnny Weissmuller had time for me. This man might well have been aloof and not had any time for me other than what was written in the script. This was not the case. Johnny Weissmuller loved me and I knew it and I loved him. When I was near, he always had a kind word for me when I might easily have passed by unnoticed. . . .

I don't like to play favorites when it comes to the movies I was in. I love them all! Bearing that in mind, *Tarzan Finds a Son!*, naturally, is my straight-ahead favorite. It was the beginning. . . . [I] rode in my first private railroad car to location in Florida; I was introduced to my fabulous tree house home; I got my own chimps to play with; I got to feed daily [for a time] Leo, the Metro Goldwyn Mayer lion; I was present when my contract was negotiated with Sam Zimbalist; and I personally picked up my first movie check! These were all firsts and wonderful events in my life that happened before and during the filming of *Tarzan Finds a Son!* . . .

I learned spiritual things from my jungle father. When I was small and learning to stand and fell, Tarzan didn't say, "Jane, Boy no good, can't stand up. Throw Boy off escarpment!" No, my jungle father helped me to stand. When I couldn't swim, my jungle dad didn't say, "Boy no good, can't swim, let him drown!" No, Tarzan taught me to swim. When Boy got out of line, Tarzan was there to point it out. "Boy, bad!" Then, in a twinkle of "Dad's" eye, I was forgiven, and we went on to experience more of this life adventure.

From these events, I learned spiritual values. From the things I could see, feel, hear, and touch, I learned about what I could not see, feel, hear, or touch. I learned that I had a spiritual father who loved me and that I could always count on him for guidance and protection; all I had to do was call. I learned then, and know now, when and how to call for backup. Thank God.

This was a special time in my life, and all of it made a lasting beginning for me in the movies—and that's why *Tarzan Finds a Son!* is my favorite Tarzan movie.

Kind words from my "brother," Johnny Sheffield. He also said that he and Big John shared a lot of laughs during the time that they worked together. For instance, they laughed together over the following story.

In Germany, during the early years of World War II, the Nazi forces occupying Freidorf, Romania, checked their records thoroughly (something for which the Germans are famous), and they discovered that one Janos (Johann) Weiszmueller had never registered for the draft. They went to see the local *burghermeister* and demanded to know his whereabouts. The mayor told them that he knew exactly where Johann Weiszmueller was. He was at the local theater at this very moment, with his boy. Nazi storm troopers burst into the theater a few minutes later. Rousting people from their seats, they demanded to know where this man named Johann Weiszmueller was. Almost en masse, the crowd turned and pointed to the screen. And there he was: Johnny Weissmuller, in a film called *Tarzan Finds a Son!*

Funny story. Sheffield probably knows more about my father's lighthearted days than I do. Unfortunately, I know more about my father's pain-filled days than Sheffield does. But those bad days were not yet even on the horizon. At this stage of his life, Johnny Weissmuller could do no wrong. The world was his oyster, and he was about to meet and marry the girl of his dreams.

Beryl Scott

After the Lupe fiasco, Dad decided to join the world of men, and to hell with women. He obtained a membership at the Lakeside Golf Club and started golfing regularly with Bob Hope, Bing Crosby, Jack Oakie, and other film celebrities. In fact, most of Dad's free time was spent on the golf links, and he eventually became an excellent golfer, shooting consistently in the seventies. He was a cheating four to six, and he could have played to a two. I have seen his golfing trophies, and they are impressive. Johnny Weissmuller made the cut at every Pro-Am tournament in which he played, including those at Pebble Beach—that miserable, rainy, foggy, windswept promontory. He could easily have turned professional, but there was no money to be made in golf in those days.

It was on the golf course, during a tournament held at Pebble Beach, that Dad met his third wife and my mother, Beryl Scott. (That is the only version of her first name that I knew her to use, but I have numerous legal records in my possession with her signature appearing as "Beryel." In many published accounts, her name is also spelled that way. I will use "Beryl" in this book.) She was twenty-one; he was thirty-five. As it had been with Grandmother Elizabeth and Grandfather Petrus, the chemistry was there. Beryl was a San Francisco socialite, but she had been born in Toronto, Canada. Her father (my Grandpa Scott) was a successful dealer in Oriental carpets. His business, located in San Francisco, was called the Turko-Persian Rug Company.

Once (I think on a fishing trip to Acapulco), I asked my father how he had met and married my mother. "Through Jon Konigshofer," he told me. "He introduced us on a golf course."

I was amazed. I knew Jon well, but I never realized that he was the man who had introduced my parents to each other. Jon had built many of the fine homes on Seventeen Mile Drive in Pebble Beach. And in Carmel, a Konigshofer house is *the* thing to own. He also built homes in Acapulco for Mexican presidents and members of their cabinets. Many, many years later, to my considerable surprise and delight, Jon married my mother.

Dad went on to say,

When I first met your mother, I realized that I didn't like being a bachelor anymore. I wanted to settle down with a real lady and have children. I wanted a family. I proposed, Beryl accepted, and the next thing I knew we were looking at building sites for our new home. It was that fast.

We bought on a lot in Brentwood, next door to Joan Crawford's home, on Bristol Street. We were only engaged, but we were so confident in our contracted marriage that we even hired architects and started construction of the house. I was happy. This was it! This would be my last marriage, and the beginning of a new life. I was determined to build one hell of a tree house for me and my family. The lonely days were over!

Dad met Lupe Vélez one last time, in Toots Shor's restaurant, where he was having lunch with Ed Sullivan. I read about this encounter in a newspaper clipping that I found in Grandmother Elizabeth's scrapbook. According to the article, Lupe approached my father's table and said, "John-ee, I reeed in the papers that you are goeeng to marry a nice society girl. Eeet eees true?"

"Yes, eeet eees true."

"But she weel be no fun for you, Pop-ee!"

"Lupe, you can keep the fun. I've had all the fun that I can handle—with you. Now I just want peace."

"Poor John-ee. You do not know that peace comes only in the grave?"

The Glory Years

My father was upset over his divorce from Lupe, but not for long. Other exciting things were looming on the horizon. By 1939, his salary at MGM had risen to $2,500 a week. The Tarzan films were being spaced further and further apart, but Dad received his salary regardless. Studio executives thought that this was a bit extravagant, so they "rented" Tarzan to Billy Rose for five thousand dollars a week to appear in his Aquacade at the New York World's Fair. Tarzan continued to draw his regular salary, and MGM pocketed the difference. All parties were happy with the arrangement.

"Well, almost," Dad said. "I had been suffering from an ear infection for some time, and my daily water routines at the Aquacade were so extensive that the problem arose again. It wasn't something incapacitating, but it was a constant annoyance. What the hell—the money was still coming in, and I got to work with Eleanor Holm—not only pretty but another Olympic champion. It was actually more fun than making movies."

On August 20, 1939, Johnny Weissmuller and Beryl Scott were married in Garfield, New Jersey. The town's mayor officiated. Sherman Billingsley—owner of the Stork Club in New York—was best man. Later that day, Dad had to hurry off for his daily Aquacade performance—actually, there were four of them. The following week, he sent this telegram to MGM: "If you want me to

Johnny goofing around with Groucho Marx and a trio of Aquabelles at the Billy Rose Aquacade of 1939, New York.

continue as Tarzan, you must get me out of the Aquacade. My doctor informs me that I'll lose my hearing if I go on giving [four] daily shows."

That resulted in an immediate release for my father, and Buster Crabbe replaced him in the Aquacade. Dad did, however, work one more time for Billy Rose, at the San Francisco World's Fair Aquacade on Treasure Island the following year. Eleanor Holm (who later married Billy Rose) elected to stay in New York, and she was replaced as Dad's swimming partner by a new young hopeful: Esther Williams.

During this time, it was confirmed that Beryl was pregnant. Dad flew her to San Francisco and installed her in a hotel, where she remained under the constant care of a doctor. He was very excited at the prospect of becoming a father, and he was taking no chances. San Francisco columnist Herb Caen heard about Beryl's pregnancy and wrote something to the effect that the kid would probably be born on a cocktail table. Dad was enraged. He went from bar to bar searching for Caen.

Later, Dad said to me, "Yeah, we were on the cocktail circuit, because that was part and parcel of the Aquacade routine, and about the only time that I got to see my wife was after working hours, at a cocktail party. Beryl was a cultivated lady, and Herb Caen made her look like a barfly! If I could have found the bastard, I would probably have wrung his neck . . . too."

I was confused. "Too? You mean also? Who else's neck . . . ?"

"Oh," he cut in, looking a bit shamefaced, "I never told you the story about Gary [the parrot]? I guess not. Don't like to talk about that. Still feel bad about that."

My father never forgave Caen, and Caen (who took great pains to hide from Big John) never lost an opportunity to gouge him in print. The feud lasted so long that even I became involved. Years later, Herb Caen often treated me shabbily in his column, to the point that I once threatened to sue him. We made peace just before his death.

As it turned out, I was not born on a cocktail table. On September 23, 1940, I was born on a perfectly respectable bed in the

Stanford Hospital in San Francisco. My sisters, Wendy Anne and Heidi Elizabeth, were born June 1, 1942, and July 31, 1944, respectively, and we moved into a larger house on Rockingham, overlooking Mandeville Canyon. But it wasn't a house; it was a mansion.

It was a mansion on a par with the mansions of Dad's buddies, Errol Flynn, Humphrey Bogart, John Wayne, Raoul Walsh, and Forrest Tucker. Together they formed the original Hollywood rat pack, and they all lived like kings. They simply had the best of everything: the best toys; the best clothing; the best parties; the best clubs; and the most beautiful women. They were the trendsetters, and everyone wanted to be associated with them, to be a part of this social phenomenon. Johnny Weissmuller was the leader of the pack. Many of Dad's former associates in that crowd told me, "Man, your daddy was the coolest dude in town."

All of this was made possible by the full approval of MGM, of course. The studio liked its stars and their spouses to look good in public. Beryl said that she had all of her makeup custom blended by the studio; these cosmetics were of the highest quality, and the colors were beautiful. Studio makeup artists used real pearls in their foundations and eyeshadows, and nothing remotely comparable to them was available on the market. Beryl's clothing was also the very best that money could buy, and she and Johnny decorated their homes with the finest of household furnishings. They lived a rarefied existence.

Stuz Bearcats, Dusenbergs, Lincoln Continentals, Cadillacs; my parents had them all. And there was the Cord, too. Dad bought Beryl the Cord shortly after they were married, but she never liked it. It had a steering wheel almost as large as the spare tire, and it didn't have power steering. She made Dad park it outside the garages, on the circular drive, so that she would not have to back it out. The house, however, was located on a dead-end street, and she still had to take it to the end of the street and horse it around in order to get it out to the main thoroughfare. I can't imagine anybody hating a Cord, but Beryl sure did. Her favorite car was a Ford woodie—its vintage was about 1942, I think. She kept that car for many years, until long after she and Dad were divorced.

Beryl and Johnny Jr., 1941.

The only car I remember, besides the Ford woodie, was a big Lincoln Continental. It was sleek and black with a white top. The doors had push buttons instead of handles, and they opened backwards. The car appeared to me to be about nine miles long. Dad never used cars in an ostentatious manner. Cars were not status symbols to him; they were simply a means of getting back and forth to work. The only chauffeur my parents had was the Duke, the man who captained Dad's yacht. The Duke was also on call as a handyman around the house.

These were good years for my parents—glory years, in fact. Unfortunately, there were all too few of them.

After World War II commenced, especially during 1942 and 1943, it became clear that the honeymoon was over. Dad didn't get to spend much time with us in our new home, because he was constantly on tour with such celebrities as Bing Crosby, Bob Hope, Bette Davis, Joan Crawford, and Buster Keaton. They were raising money for the war effort.

Johnny Weissmuller's age and the fact that he had children kept him out of active service, but he made up for it by helping to raise millions of dollars for the cause. He even washed dishes at the Hollywood Canteen. Furthermore, as well as nostalgic music and other familiar sounds from home, American GIs were requesting that Weissmuller's Tarzan yell be broadcast on the battlefront. For two years, Dad taught navy recruits how to swim to safety from beneath waters covered in flaming petroleum, a service that earned him a special citation from the U.S. War Finance Program in 1945. In the process, Dad got singed a few times, but more often he was singed by mother for taking such foolish risks. Beryl was very upset with him.

It wasn't just the demands of contributing to the war effort that caused marital discord in the Weissmuller household; it was also the demands of the film business. Dad was almost never home: *Tarzan's Secret Treasure* and *Tarzan's New York Adventure* were filmed back

Beryl with Wendy and Heidi, 1944.

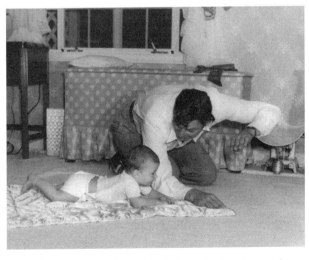

Johnny Sr. prepping little Johnny Jr. for the pool.

to back, and this was compounded by the fact that MGM dropped the Tarzan series in 1942 and RKO Pathe picked it up. Those involved had to move and set up shop in an entirely new environment. At RKO, they shot *Tarzan Triumphs* in 1943, followed immediately (in the same year) by *Tarzan's Desert Mystery*.

The change of studio was prompted by the fact that in 1942 MGM's option with Edgar Rice Burroughs expired, and studio executives did not want to renew the contract because of dwindling returns from foreign markets due to the war. Another factor was that the budget for the Tarzan series had been cut after the death of Irving Thalberg, who had been a champion of that project. But, for whatever reason, the Tarzan contract was up for grabs, and the ubiquitous Hollywood Pied Piper Sol Lesser came out of the woodwork and grabbed it. Armed with the blessing of Edgar Rice Burroughs, Weissmuller's contract, and young Johnny Sheffield, Lesser promptly moved the entire Tarzan cast and crew over to Culver City, where RKO Pathe was located.

When it came to luxury features, RKO was in no way comparable to MGM. The front office was built to look like a grand Southern plantation house, but it was only a front. The soundstages were located just behind the main offices, and behind that lay the back lot. The big differences between MGM and RKO were all related to size and luxury. Working at RKO was apparently rough at first—it was hard to learn the ropes and the rules—but the Tarzan cast and crew gradually worked their way through the problems, and they came to enjoy working in the studio's more relaxed and informal atmosphere. Many of the actors, and even members of the film crew, wore nothing but bathing suits at work most of the time.

RKO Pathe had many other things going for it. It had a matte department second to none, a "jungle" and a lake on its forty-acre back lot, and an Arab village that had been built for the film *The Garden of Allah*. Four of the six Johnny Weissmuller RKO films were shot around that location. Another RKO Pathe bonus was the fact that it owned fifty percent of Churubusco Studios in Mexico. The Tarzan project saved a lot of time and money when shooting on location in Mexico because it had the use of the Churubusco facility: this was especially helpful in the case of my father's last Tarzan film, *Tarzan and the Mermaids*, which was shot in Acapulco.

Paul Stader, Dad's stunt double, performed the dive from the cliff at Lake Sherwood for *Tarzan Triumphs*, and thirteen years later he executed a similar dive at the same spot while doubling for my father as Jungle Jim in the TV series. Paul did most of the stunts for my father during the Tarzan days, usually because Dad just wanted to give Paul a "bump."

Back then, stuntmen worked for a daily rate. When they did a stunt, they got what they called a "bump"—a bonus equal to half a day's pay. So, if they did two bumps, they got an extra full day's pay. Paul once did a long aerial stunt for Dad in a Tarzan movie, swinging on a vine between two trees. The rope broke, sending Paul on a fast track to the ground. It nearly killed him, but he did recover fully. After that, Dad gave Paul bumps all the time. He would often do a stunt and then say, "Ah, I didn't like that one, let's have Paul do it." Payback for a favor done.

Paul and his wife, Marilyn, became my father's lifelong friends and mine also. Paul died a few years ago, but we still keep in touch with Marilyn. Friends like that one tries never to lose.

As I said earlier, the move to RKO and the accelerated filming of the Tarzan movies took their toll on my parents' marriage. My father fulfilled the demands of his work schedule, and at home my mother became restless. Dad was almost never there, and she couldn't find domestic help during the war years, since likely candidates were all off being "Rosie the Riveter," building tanks or ships or whatever; they were making three times the money they had earned as maids. Even offers of raises didn't help. They had a war to win!

So on the domestic front the war was not going well at all. Mother began to bring to the house her high-society friends; Dad began to spend more time at work or on the golf course; they were each jealous of the other's friendships. When Mother decided to sell the oversized mansion in which we were living due to the shortage of domestic help, Dad was furious.

What little social life my parents still shared usually involved

Dad's sailing partners. They partied with Humphrey Bogart and his wife, Mayo, and those two fought in private and public just as much as Dad and Lupe Vélez had done. One night, Dad and Beryl went to pick them up, and they found Bogie waving a gun and threatening to kill Mayo. Mother said, "Bogie was drunk, out of his mind, and obviously a dangerous man. Without batting an eye, John walked over to Bogie and calmly removed the gun from his hand. Your father and I had our differences, but I can say for a fact that the man was totally without fear—of anything. I wonder if the animals he worked with sensed that too?"

I later asked Dad to confirm that story, and he said, "Yeah, I guess so. More or less." After thinking about it for a moment, he added, "I always liked Bogie. He was fun to be around—when he wasn't with Mayo, when he was just one of the guys. But Mayo was a lot like Beryl. Neither one of them were much fun to be around for long. Get-togethers might start out okay, but sooner or later one of those two would start a fight about something. It's like hanging around someone who always has a runny nose and is always sneezing. Sooner or later, you're going to catch something." "Tarzan" had a knack for getting right to the nub of a problem.

Years later, long after my parents had divorced, Mother told me another story about Mayo and Bogie: "I felt so sorry for Mayo. In 1944, she and I were together watching the rushes of the first Humphrey Bogart–Lauren Bacall film, *To Have and Have Not,* and Mayo started sobbing and shaking uncontrollably. Bogie was forty-five, and Bacall was twenty-two, but Mayo saw them on-screen, sensed the chemistry, and knew that that was the beginning of the end for her and Bogie."

Dad said that his marital problems with Beryl came to a head when she heard from bridge partners Connie Baker, Irene Ryan, Patty Lake, and Monica Pokinghorn that Dad's business manager, Bö (pronounced Boo) Roos, was stealing from him. Beryl confronted Dad with this information, and Dad confronted Roos. Roos told

Dad that the problem lay with his wife: she was spending entirely too much money. "Besides," Roos said, "women know little or nothing about the intricacies of finance. Trust me, Johnny, this is much ado about nothing!"

Dad told Beryl what Roos had said, and the fight must have been a real wall banger, because immediately thereafter he left home. I believe it was in December 1943. The marriage did not officially end at that point. Divorce proceedings continued for another five years, and the court battles over property and custody issues became increasingly vindictive. But all that Wendy, Heidi, and I knew about it was that after 1943 we no longer had a father.

Rattrap

I was sure that I had lost my father because of a rattrap. I have only vague recollections of the day Dad left home, but my mother told me that at the time we were living at number 2 Latimer Road in Santa Monica Canyon. Dad apparently reached behind a shelf, and a rattrap snapped on his finger. It started bleeding profusely. He yelled so loudly that it frightened me, and then he and Mother got into a shouting match. One thing led to another, and they began accusing each other of things that I did not understand. I was scared to death. Dad stormed out of the house, never to return. I was about three and a half years old, and the next time I saw my father was in 1953, when I was thirteen. My sisters and I were left behind, sentenced to live with my mother in the house on Latimer.

And Mother was not easy to live with. She was anything but a perfect mom. She was a fantastic backgammon and bridge player, and she used to leave Wendy, Heidi, and me on the beach at the Santa Monica Beach Club while she played with the "girls." I remember a family story (often repeated over the years, I think merely to emphasize Beryl's sense of intense concentration) concerning Wendy. She ran up from the beach one day to Mother with a dead mole on the top of her head. Mother glanced briefly at her and, not even shifting her cards, said, "That's nice, dear. Two hearts!"

Mother would become so preoccupied with social events that she actually lost Wendy on one occasion. Every Saturday morning, the mothers of the Weissmuller, Donohue, Middleton, Muñoz, and Field families took their children, numbering about eight in all, to the Hitching Post Theater and left them there until around four in the afternoon. It was an all-day affair. The mothers took turns dropping off and picking up the kids. One Saturday evening, about sundown, we sat down to dinner, and Mother realized that Wendy was not there. She said, "Oh, my God!," jumped up from the table, and roared off in the Ford woodie. She found Wendy sitting on the sidewalk, unharmed and sobbing. When they got home, Heidi and I exchanged smug looks. Our "Nursie" and mother always favored Wendy because she had a club foot. Heidi and I got the banging around. Wendy was always the poor little broken-winged sparrow. I guess Heidi and I just forgot to mention that Wendy was missing.

I'm not keen on self-analysis. I'm not keen on trying to analyze other people. I'm not keen on excusing inappropriate behavior of any sort on the basis of childhood abuse and the possible resultant trauma. But I have been thinking about Wendy lately, and I have to face the fact that the mole incident, which everyone had laughed off as a simple joke, was not a joke at all. It was my sister's desperate attempt to be recognized. She was catapulted from the arms of a warm, adoring father to an uninterested mother whose primary loves were a bridge table and a cocktail party. To this day, Wendy has emotional problems, and neither Heidi nor I escaped unscathed.

Losing our father was bad enough. Losing our mother to her social circle was just about the last straw. It affected all of us. Wendy developed the habit of tearing out her hair and eating it. Heidi developed a lisp, and I developed a stutter, which I had until I was a grown man. I have had to face the fact that our mother simply did not like children. Later on in life, she did not even like her grandchildren. I have come to the conclusion that there may be something to the oft-repeated speculation that English mothers are, on the whole, basically cold and detached. There are exceptions, of course, and Beryl could sometimes be one. There were occasions when she became almost maudlin in her dedication to—and defense of—her family. Strange woman. Strange mother.

The only time that Beryl ever mentioned Dad's name in those ten years my sisters and I went without seeing him was during the period immediately after his departure. She explained to us that she and Dad would no longer be living together, but that he was still our father, and he would be visiting us on Sundays. I remember vividly that every Sunday she dressed my sisters and me in our best clothes and seated us in the foyer of the house. For hours I waited in quiet anticipation for Tarzan to come through the door. With every sound I heard coming from outside the door, I imagined his six-foot-four-inch frame approaching, my excitement building, only to feel it fade to disappointment. The sound I heard was never Tarzan. Sunday after Sunday, he never came. I would even go outside and sit on the curb, looking up and down the street, but he never came. Mother always said the same thing: "Well, he didn't come again! As usual, probably off fooling around with some other woman!"

It was years later before I learned, from Dad, that he was sitting across town all that time, hoping for a phone call permitting him to visit us. Mother had somehow won a restraining order prohibiting him from seeing his children. If he had come to the house without court approval, or without mother's approval, she could have put him in jail. She *wanted* to put him in jail! She was using his children as bait! It is hard to say, but I don't think, in my heart, that I ever really forgave my mother for that.

All those years, I was convinced that my father simply did not want to see me, that he really didn't love me, that perhaps somehow I had let him down. Had Boy from the Tarzan series taken my place? Sometimes I imagined so. I was always a bit envious of Johnny Sheffield, who was Weissmuller's Boy in many Tarzan films. He was "raised" by my father, while I was raised by my mother. Later in life, I saw Boy and Jane and *my* father—a happy family unit— on-screen. I wished I could have shared that bliss. My boyhood was not all that tragic, but I felt somehow crippled by not having a dad around like other kids. When I finally found my Old Man again, we worked hard together to make up for what we had lost during those critical boyhood years.

⌒

In 1944, Lupe Vélez reentered the scene, tragically. Her tumultuous affairs had often been mentioned in the newspapers, and during one of those affairs she became pregnant. Word spread rapidly around Hollywood (as it always does) that the prospective father was an actor named Harald Ramond and that he had refused to marry her. Several times, Lupe had called my mother to make an appointment to talk with her—they had come to know each other well because they traveled in the same social circles, and, of course, they had Johnny Weissmuller in common. Lupe had divorced him, and by 1944 Beryl was involved in divorce proceedings herself. Lupe needed to talk to somebody, anybody. She was panicked and needed advice. My mother didn't have time for her, and a few days later Lupe killed herself.

How did Lupe die? The stories are many and varied. One account has her dying in bed from an overdose of drugs. My parents both told me that they had heard that she died with her head in a toilet bowl. But that's about all they knew. They didn't know the details. Nobody seemed to know the details.

Bill Reed was fortunate enough to talk with Bö Roos's daughter, Carolyn Roos Olsen, recently, and she gave him the following account of the death of Lupe Vélez, which I am convinced is pretty accurate:

The story about how Lupe Vélez died has been told many times, and in many ways, but never exactly the way that it happened. Lupe wanted a child so much, but when this actor named Harald Ramond got her pregnant, he wouldn't marry her. She called everybody, asking for help and advice, and one of those persons was my father, Bö Roos. Lupe was part of Dad's "stable" of stars, and he was also very fond of her, so he arranged for Lupe to go down to Acapulco and stay with her sister, have the baby there, and then come back to the States. After an appropriate period of time, she would return to Acapulco and "adopt" the baby.

This was all set up, and it is what Lupe wanted to do. Well, she obviously changed her mind and decided, from what Dad deduced, to try one last time with Ramond and try to get him to marry her. She called him, set up an appointment for him to come to her house, arranged the house with flowers and candles and all, and dressed in a lovely negligee. Then, whether to calm herself or to scare Harald Ramond (we don't know), she took sleeping pills, and, before he arrived, she got sick to her stomach and died throwing up in the toilet.

Lupe's housekeeper phoned my father immediately upon discovering her body, and he rushed over to her house with his nephew, Charlie Trebon (who worked for him at the time), and a doctor. This broke Dad's heart. He so loved Lupe Vélez. He got hold of Police Chief Anderson of the Beverly Hills Police Department, and Anderson agreed to hush up the entire thing. He put a lid on the story. This was not unusual in those days. The police would often call Dad in the middle of the night when one of his stars was in trouble, and he would go right down and take care of the problem, and it never hit the newspapers. That is one of the reasons why there is still so much mystery, and so many unanswered questions, about this tragic incident.

As I said, Lupe's death really broke Dad's heart, and he made arrangements for a memorial to be erected for her in San Luis Potosí, Mexico, where she had been born. Dad had to erect this special monument in a private plot, because the Catholic Church looked on this as a suicide and would not let her be buried in sacred ground. Dad hired someone to take care of the monument for life and also arranged for someone to replace the caretaker after he died. That's the way my father told the story to me, and I have no reason to disbelieve it.

The public held Harald Ramond responsible for Lupe's death, and he never worked in films again. There are many people in Hollywood who think that this was unjust. The story goes that Ramond took the heat for Lupe's baby, which was actually Gary Cooper's. I once went to Universal Studios with Diane to attend a Screen Actors Guild meeting, and while we were there Diane met Lupe's former hairdresser (who also did Lupe's hair for her funeral). He said that Lupe told him that the baby was Cooper's, and we know that no one lies to her hairdresser. I wouldn't be a bit surprised if what the man said was true. Beryl always suspected as much. Anyway, poor old Harald was ridden out of town on a rail.

Dad said that after Lupe's death he thought often about that conversation they'd had at Toots Shor's back in 1939, when Lupe had said, "Poor John-ee. You do not know that peace comes only in the grave?" He said that he realized early on what a sad and tormented woman Lupe Vélez was, but he always cared about her.

Meanwhile, the Hollywood castle of the Weissmuller dynasty was rumbling and tumbling. What has always amazed me is just how fast those heady, happy, glory days for Dad and Beryl came and went. They had enjoyed only a little more than four years together.

Everyone always assumed, as did we children, that my mother had been the one to file for divorce. It was many years later, during conversations I had with Dad, that I realized he was the plaintiff and Mother the defendant. I have the divorce document in my possession. Dad also showed me files from a private detective agency he had employed to shadow my mother, and these establish the fact that she was playing around rather heavily: meeting strange men, driving to out-of-the-way spots up in the hills, and reemerging hours later. True? Apparently the judge thought so—he ruled in favor of my father.

The divorce decree, dated January 29, 1948, reads: "... the Court, having been fully advised in the premises, and having duly

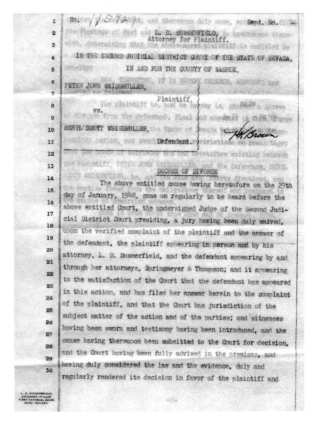

Johnny's decree of divorce from Beryl.

considered the law and the evidence, duly and regularly rendered its decision in favor of the plaintiff and against the defendant . . . determining that the . . . plaintiff [Peter John Weissmuller] is entitled to a decree of divorce from the defendant [Beryl Scott Weissmuller] on the grounds of extreme cruelty. . . ."

These are not easy things to reveal about one's mother, but, in all fairness, I think that the truth should be told. So who was more in the wrong, Beryl or Johnny Weissmuller? Let God be the judge. I don't want that job. There was more than enough blame to go around. In the meantime, life went on, and my father continued to make headline news.

"An Alfred Hitchcock Erotic Nightmare!"

There is no doubt in my mind: Johnny Weissmuller was no saint. I think that at one point Dad began to believe that he really *was* Tarzan. Careless "prey," whether in the African jungle or the Hollywood jungle, was fair game. At least that's the aura that grew up around him; that's what the public wanted to believe.

This brings to mind statements made by Esther Williams in her recent book. She described Johnny Weissmuller as being "well endowed." When asked what she meant by that in interviews, she replied, in effect, "Well, if you're going to *play* Tarzan, you had best *be* Tarzan."

Esther Williams has made numerous derogatory remarks about my father in magazine articles and during talk-show appearances over the past few years. The most recent was in January 2002, on a news program about the World's Fair. My wife went to her pharmacist to get a prescription filled, and he said that he was outraged by the malicious things that Esther Williams was saying about Johnny Weissmuller. It came as no surprise. I do recall that in her book Esther claimed that my mother once approached her and asked if she was having an affair with my father. I am a bit skeptical of that story. Knowing Mom as I do, I can assure you that if she had even vaguely suspected Dad of having an affair with Esther Williams, or with anyone else, she would have hired a private detective and hauled my father's ass into court. She would never have demeaned herself by asking the other woman about it, thereby admitting that a man might actually be getting the better of her. My mother played only hardball.

On the fiftieth anniversary of the Billy Rose Aquacades at Treasure Island, I rode in a parade car with Esther Williams. Diane was waiting for me with Esther's grandchildren; they were being chaperoned by an impressive young man. Diane is most discriminating in her choice of friends, but she liked this guy immediately, and they began to talk. The conversation turned to my father, and the young man said that Esther had told him that Big John couldn't keep his hands off her. Diane refrained from commenting that it was probably because he had to teach her how to swim. Anyway, that sounds like the same thing we hear when she intimates on talk shows that every man she has ever met falls in love with her. Trying to change the subject tactfully, Diane said that Esther must be proud to have such a charming son. The young man said, "I am not her son. I am her fiancé."

Chuckling later about that faux pas, Diane said to me, "I'm usually a bit more discreet than that."

No one can dispute the fact that Esther Williams has always had a large male following, but looking at the scoreboard one also wonders if she has ever really *liked* men. This old hay bag (that's what people in Hollywood have always called her—I'm not sure if she knows this or even cares) apparently still thinks of herself as a femme fatale, and she has been most unkind in print to her ex-husbands. She made a big to-do about Jeff Chandler being a cross-dresser; for no apparent reason other than the need to spread malicious gossip, she besmirched his reputation. Esther also had denigrating things to say about Fernando Lamas. She claimed that he would drive around naked from the waist down so as not to ruin the crease in his trousers.

In the April 2000 issue of *Architectural Digest,* Esther said that when she was in the Aquacades, she found that Billy Rose's advances were easy to resist but that Weissmuller's were harder. During every show, she said, the King of the Jungle whipped off his bathing suit and, out of sight of the audience, groped her underwater. She described it as "an Alfred Hitchcock erotic nightmare!"

When I read that account of my father whipping off his bathing suit and exposing himself, I thought of a story that Mother had told me: "Your father always wore this beautiful monogrammed robe at the Billy Rose Aquacade. One night, he climbed up to the diving board, opened his robe, and almost dropped it when he discovered that he had forgotten to put on his bathing suit. He was absolutely mortified!"

Beryl told me often that Dad was a very proper, modest man. That's one reason that the narcissistic and wanton behavior of Lupe Vélez drove him up the wall. That is also one of the reasons that I think Esther Williams protests too much. I find it hard to believe that she ever really had much, if anything, going with "Tarzan."

Mike Oliver—Dad's close friend and confidant, who owned and operated the *Acapulco News* and was also a UPI correspondent in Acapulco—said recently that he also doubted that my father ever had an affair with Esther Williams.

> Hell, he didn't even like her. He told me on numerous occasions that Esther Williams was an average swimmer, and the only reason she was chosen to replace Eleanor Holm as his costar in the Aquacades was because he told Billy Rose to give him the tallest girl in the Aquabelles; not the best, but the *tallest*. Johnny said she had an awkward swimming style, lacking in power and form, until he coached her. What ticked him off was the fact that Esther Williams never once gave him credit for that.

I am not calling Esther a liar. Only she knows the truth about that, since, conveniently for her, Weissmuller Sr. is dead. Like Jeff Chandler and Fernando Lamas, he is not around to defend himself. I, on the other hand, am quite capable of commenting, and in light of the foregoing and many other published and televised attacks by Esther Williams against my father, I have no reservations about defending his honor.

As I see it, my father was an innocent with a very healthy libido. I fully agree with my "brother," Johnny Sheffield, that Dad was a man of great heart and courage and principle. Passion? Yeah, he had that too, and when women stampeded over him he may have had his weak moments, but that did not make him a womanizer. And it most certainly did not make him one of "Alfred Hitchcock's erotic nightmares." It made him Tarzan.

CHAPTER 5

Surges

Weissmuller's story should be read by all prospective actors, for it represents a textbook
case of innocence exploited and ultimately lost.

—Mark Goodman

I don't know exactly when Dad started hitting the bottle, but I
suspect it was during the Lupe Vélez period. I do know that he got
into that scene pretty heavily following his divorce from Beryl. He
was depressed, and in an effort to get his mind off his domestic
problems, he partied hard and spent money with careless abandon.

At the urging of Bö Roos, Dad bought an apartment building in
Beverly Hills. Later, he joined Red Skelton, Robert Walker, Frank
Borzage, Merle Oberon, Harriet Parsons, Joan Crawford, and John
Wayne as investors in a beach club venture named the California
Cabaña (Deauville) Club in Santa Monica. The place had several
bars and both indoor and outdoor swimming pools, and it featured
the best bands of the era for musical entertainment and dancing.
The venture lasted a few years, but it eventually went bust. The

California Cabaña Club was simply ahead of its time. The world was not yet ready for beach clubs.

The next investment, the California Country Club, which included a golf course, was a success, but only in a limited way because the eight investors—including Dad and most of the other California Cabaña Club investors—did not have enough money to expand and promote it properly. Bö Roos tried to interest the 150 or so club members to invest as well—if they had, there would have been enough money to run the place properly. But the members voted against it, so Roos and the other investors decided to sell the whole operation, golf course and all, to a land developer, who then built houses on the golf-course land. I think the investors all made a little money on that deal, but not much.

The California Country Club was near the Westside Tennis Club. The Country Club investors group, Dad among them, also owned that establishment, but in those days there was no real money in tennis clubs. Tennis players were not paid what they are today, and the clubs did not draw the crowds. It seems that Roos's ideas were always a bit ahead of their time. For example, the Polar Pantry—a frozen-meat-locker venture involving many of the same investors and located on Fred MacMurray's ranch—also failed to make it.

These were just some of the investments my father and his friends got themselves into. Some turned out great; some didn't. It was quite a gamble, but back then it was better than playing the stock market. And one thing that Roos always did was have his investors buy apartment buildings and, if possible, live in them; they could then use them as tax write-offs.

One day, while we were sitting around in Dad's den having a bull session, he said to me,

Our thoughts about the California Cabaña Club and other investments at the time were "win some, lose some." All of the investors with Roos had plenty of money—or so I thought. Bö had made a couple of bad investments. Hell, nobody could bat a thousand! Roos handled everything, of course, as he handled all my financial deals. I trusted him implicitly. So I lost a few bucks. Big deal. I still had a good salary and collected an additional $75,000 for making *Swamp Fire* for Pine and Thomas, which was underwritten by Paramount Studios. Buster Crabbe and I wrestled underwater for a few scenes, and both came out wet but richer. Money? I never thought about money. I was confident that I had enough in the bank, and in good investments by Roos, that I could spend what I wanted for the rest of my life. If not, I could always make more. I was popular. Everybody said so.

Dad shuffled through his memorabilia papers and came up with a clipping. He said, "Here, look at this!" It was an article from the *Los Angeles Herald Express*, written by George T. Davis:

A group of us were talking at Lakeside [golf course] the other day—including Fred Cady, Pat McCormick, Maurie Luxford, John Farrington, Bob Ford, Tom Russell, Dutch Smith, and Jimmy McLauren—and Cady, probably the greatest swimming authority in the world, [said] "They broke the mold with Weissmuller. He was Mr. Swimming himself and there's never been anyone like him. I don't care whether his records are broken or not, Johnny was by far the greatest of 'em all. He had power, form, and competitive ability to a greater degree than any swimmer of the time and ranks in his sport along with such other champions as Bobby Jones, Bill Tilden, Babe Ruth, and Jack Dempsey.

Dad retrieved the clipping, grinned at me, and said, "See? I was rich and famous! Sportswriters liked me—and, especially, girls liked me."

Allene Gates

One of those girls was a teenager named Allene Gates. And, as with Beryl, it all started on a golf course. In fact, it was on the golf course of the California Country Club, of which Dad was then part owner, and of which Bö Roos was vice president.

Allene Gates, Johnny's third wife.

Dad said that there was a player who came to the club's golf course nicknamed "3-Iron" Gates. They called him that because of a car accident in which he had ruined his back. In those days, golfers didn't use golf carts; they carried their bags on their backs. Gates couldn't do that, so he carried only a 3-iron (this was mostly at the Fox Hills Country Club, but he also frequented the California Country Club, where Dad first met him). Gates would hustle guys by saying, "I'll bet you I can beat you with only one club!"

Dad said that Gates made lots of money. One of his gambits was to put a leaf behind his ball and say, "This gives it loft." I suppose a pro would call that an "assisted" overspin. Gates always "lofted" the ball exactly where he wanted it. He had a few tricks up his sleeve, but my father assured me that he was not a crook—he was simply a damned good golfer who happened to have a bad back. He compensated. Dad liked the guy a lot. His daughter, Allene, often played with him, and one day my father found himself teamed up with her in a foursome. He and Allene won. The girl was ecstatic, and after that they played together often. Dad recalled Allene during one of our discussions about women:

It started out as no more than a casual friendship. Actually, more like a father-daughter relationship. Hell, her father was about my age! But when I say she was a "teenager," I mean at least very late teens. She sure as hell didn't look, or act, like a teenager.

One thing led to another: Allene couldn't swim well, so I taught her. Many things threw us together, and soon we actually started dating. Then the newspapers picked up on that, and I remember thinking, "Christ! That's all I need! Beryl and her lawyers are going to love this!" I happily accepted the chance to go on location in Acapulco and make *Tarzan and the Mermaids* with Linda Christian—someone a bit more adult.

Allene gave the following version of how she came to meet and marry my father:

*A young Allene watches as her friend and the future
Female Athlete of the Half Century, Babe Didrikson Zaharias,
hits the ball out of the bunker.*

I was born in Ocean Park, California, but I actually spent little
time on the beach with my childhood friends. I was an only
child, and most of my life I was in the company of my parents
on a golf course. I was an adult early on because I knew only
the golf course and adult company. That is not a complaint; I
loved every minute of my brief childhood. I loved my mother
and father dearly. They were married at the ages of fifteen and
nineteen, respectively, and they had a very good marriage—
cemented by golf. I was playing golf before the age of nine and
had my first hole-in-one at the age of ten. I met your father on
the golf course when I was thirteen. I had a crush on him then,
and I never really lost it my entire life. I always pulled my

chair up next to his in the clubhouse. He would pat me on the head and joke with me until the drinks began to flow, and then he'd say, "Go find your parents, kid. Get out of here!" I always obeyed, just as I always obeyed him later in life.

I remember that one day he patted me on the head and said, "Honey, someday, after you grow up, I'm going to marry you!" Little did we know.

I met your father the second time when I was sixteen and playing in a golf tournament. I think it was at the California Country Club. He was a member there, and so was I, after becoming the southern California amateur champion. I think that is when I began to think about marrying him. Your father always said that he married a teenager, but that is not true. After your mother and father separated, he lived in an apartment upstairs at the golf club. I saw him every day, and we started playing golf and then dating when I was around nineteen . . . over my father's strenuous objection. He didn't speak to me for six months after he found out that I was dating a man who was his same age! My father and Johnny were very good friends, but Daddy definitely did not approve of our relationship.

Anyway, it worked out. We were married in 1948, when I was twenty-two and Johnny was forty-four. The marriage lasted for fifteen years. We were divorced in 1963, perhaps the saddest day of my life. I really loved Johnny Weissmuller. I wanted to live with him forever, but he eventually carried a load that I was too frail to share.

Tarzan in Acapulco

The Old Man always loved Acapulco, even before he went down there in 1948 with Sol Lesser to film *Tarzan and the Mermaids*. Everybody there knew him and loved him, and the Mexican fans followed him around in droves. I was not there with him—I was still under my mother's thumb—but Allene told me, and Mike Oliver confirmed it, that my father in those days had a star quality and a magnetism that was almost frightening in its intensity. Buddy

Rogers, appearing on a television program following Dad's death in 1984, remarked, "When Johnny Weissmuller had something to say, everyone listened. He was a compelling force."

He was that, but he was also a man who just liked to have fun. He enjoyed life to the fullest. I never remember a dull moment when I was around my father. He had a keen sense of humor, and he could take a joke without getting flustered. Mike Oliver told me a story that illustrates this point well:

> One night, your dad decided to go to La Perla in Acapulco and watch the cliff divers, since in *Tarzan and the Mermaids* there was a scene where Tarzan was supposed to dive from a cliff, and he wanted to study it. Raúl "Chupetas" García was the leader of the fourteen scheduled divers, and he dedicated his dive that night to Johnny Weissmuller. With all the lights off in the gorge below, there was complete darkness except for the lighted torches Raúl held in each hand while waiting for the precise wave to dive into—that wave would give the diver the added depth he needed to survive the plunge.
>
> Raúl was the only diver who spoke English, and when he came to the top of the steps at La Perla the audience gave him thunderous applause. Then, in English, he challenged your dad to do the dive. Your dad was deeply embarrassed, but he rose to meet the challenge. The RKO executives attending the event immediately stopped him, claiming that if anything happened hundreds of people would be out of work, the movie could not be finished, and the insurance company would not cover any accident of this sort. So your dad, who really didn't want to dive off this damned cliff anyway, sat down quite relieved. Everybody in the crowd laughed, but it didn't bother your dad at all. He just stood up, grinned, then cupped his hands to his mouth and gave off with the most ear-shattering Tarzan yell that I have ever heard. The entire crowd came to their feet in thunderous applause. Your dad really stole the show that night.

*Johnny and Allene share a laugh and some cake
on their wedding day.*

In the early 1950s, Dad, John Wayne, Red Skelton, and other members of Bö Roos's stable purchased the Los Flamingos Hotel in Acapulco. Roos, a close friend of Mexico's president, Miguel Alemán, arranged the entire thing with the presidential blessing. Present at the time was a busboy named Adolfo Santiago, who is now the owner and operator of Hotel Los Flamingos. Adolfo once told me,

> I met your father in 1950 when he came down here on a trip in his boat. Your papa, he loved Acapulco. He came here four or five times a year. In 1954, Bö Roos came to this hotel and talked with the owner. They agreed upon a price, and Roos, your papa, John Wayne, and others bought the place. They

opened it first as a private club, and then in 1960 it was opened to the public.

Those were good days in Acapulco. Wayne, Weissmuller, Frank Sinatra, Bing Crosby, even Jimmy Hoffa could walk the streets *sin problemas*. Nobody ever bothered them. Now you cannot do that. Your papa and John Wayne bought me my first guitar. I now play professionally, and I feel that I owe my talent to them.

I saw Allene when she came through here recently on a cruise boat. She was always my favorite of his wives. Very much a lady, and still *muy bonita*! It was good to see her. It brought back many fine memories.

I asked Adolfo what he thought about my father's fifth wife, María, who is still living in Acapulco. He stared at me for a long moment and then said, "No, I'd rather not say anything about María. She had best talk for herself. Yes, that is best—you talk with María about María."

~~~~

Gabriel Azcárraga, who owns and operates the Club del Sol hotel in Acapulco (as well as hotels in Mexico City, Monterrey, Puerto Vallarta, and elsewhere in Mexico), played host to Bill Reed on a recent fact-finding trip to Acapulco, along with his lovely companion, Maru Eugenia Silva. Gabriel provided Reed with transportation to interview sites and arranged a tour, on his speedboat, of the Pie de la Cuesta, where many parts of *Tarzan and the Mermaids* were filmed. He explained that a *Rambo* sequel as well as a French-Canadian Tarzan film were also filmed in that location. "It was nothing like Weissmuller's films," he added. "He was the best. Acapulco misses him very much."

Gabriel mentioned that the Tres Vidas golf course in Acapulco is one of the most exclusive in the world. The pros there told him their favorite golfing story about Dad. It happened in Cuba, just after Fidel Castro's overthrow of the Cuban government. It seems that rebel troops were rounding up and summarily executing anybody who remotely resembled a rich capitalist, and the golf course was a prime hunting ground for them. They found Johnny Weissmuller there, playing in a foursome on the thirteenth hole. They began to interrogate the golfers, one by one. When they came to Weissmuller, he grinned and said, "Me Tarzan."

Since Dad did not know how to pronounce Tarzan in Spanish ("Tarzaan"), the rebels had no idea what the hell he was talking about, and they began to prod him with their rifles. In desperation, Dad threw back his head and gave out a Tarzan yell while beating his chest. "Eeee!" shouted the rebel leader. "¡Es Tarzán! ¿Tú viste? ¡Es Tarzán de la Jungla!"

They laughed, patted him on the back, and tried to shake his hand all at the same time; then they provided him with an escort back to his hotel. These peasant troops might not have recognized the pope, but they sure as hell knew who Tarzan was.

When I told Allene that story, she said,

Boy is that ever true! Everybody in the world knew Tarzan, but you'd also be surprised how many people, perhaps especially in foreign countries, looked up to Johnny Weissmuller as the greatest swimming champion of the world. People in Europe and in many Third World countries, for example, might not follow what's going on in the movie world, but they take their sports seriously—to the point of fanaticism.

What always amazed me, even frightened me at times, was the way that people in foreign countries reacted to your father's appearance. They loved him! They loved him so much that they tried to rip the buttons off his coat. In Cairo in 1953, Nasser even showed up at one of your father's appearances with half the Egyptian army in tow. People swarmed around our car, and the soldiers beat them away with rifle butts. It was a scary experience. Johnny Weissmuller was not just a national idol; he was an international idol.

We had another, similar experience in Mexico City in 1954. The crowd literally mobbed him, just trying to touch him. We were with some other people, but we all got separated, and we lost your father completely. The crowd swallowed him up. We finally located "Tarzan" when we heard him shouting, "*Por favor,* for Christ's sake! . . . *Por favor,* for Christ's sake!"

Your father loved the Mexican people, but his Spanish was atrocious. They didn't seem to care. I suppose with the Mexicans it is only the feeling that counts.

When I say that the entire world loved Johnny Weissmuller, I mean the *entire* world, including our Cold War enemies at the time. Arlene Meuller, who was in Moscow doing an article for *Sports Illustrated* when he died, reported that the Russians played his Tarzan yell in Red Square for twenty-four hours straight. Even mainland China's state-run television reported it. Their nightly news devoted nearly four minutes to Weissmuller, showing clips of harrowing scenes from his Tarzan films.

It all seemed amazing to me at the time, but on reflection I realize how and why this all happened. Throughout the 1930s and '40s, and even into the '50s, Tarzan movies were about the hottest thing on the foreign markets. I was told that one Tarzan film ran eighteen weeks in Cairo. And in some Asiatic countries, the arrival of a new Tarzan film was the occasion for a white-tie-and-tails premiere, with the local populace fighting to get seats. In Shanghai, Bombay, and Egypt, Tarzan broke the record of all the movies released by RKO in its history. Quite a feat, considering RKO also had the Astaire–Rogers films and those of Walt Disney.

And even when the Tarzan films went out of vogue, Johnny Weissmuller *never* went out of vogue. As I said, people literally fought just to get near him. It was somewhat unnerving being married to a man like that.

⌣

When my father returned from Acapulco, he learned that his dear friend Manuel Rodríguez y Sánchez, or "Manolete," the greatest matador of all time, and a bull named Islero, had met their *hora de la verdad* together: they killed each other in Linares, Spain. Dad said, "That distressed me almost as much as the news that my days as Tarzan were over. I was getting too old to swing on vines and leap from cliffs and wrestle with alligators and lions. I was released from my contract. That really meant that I was kicked out on my ass. And as if that wasn't enough, I began receiving threats from your mother and her lawyers, and I read this in the newspapers."

He handed me another news clipping, which was a column by Louella Parsons:

> If Johnny Weissmuller is willing to pay a minimum of $600 a month and 25% of his earnings he can have his divorce from Mrs. Beryel [sic] Scott Weissmuller, from whom he has been separated for almost two years. But yesterday, Johnny refused to sign. He thought Mrs. Weissmuller's demands too exorbitant, but her attorney, Charles Katz, is holding out firmly for that amount, while Frank Belcher, representing Johnny, said the demands are out of all reason. According to Bö Roos, who manages Johnny, Mrs. Weissmuller has been given a counter-offer of 25% of his earnings with all doctor bills for the children taken care of, and the house and furniture. "Johnny hasn't a job," said Bö, "so how can he pay $600 a month?" Johnny wants the divorce so he'll be free to marry Allene Gates, but Mrs. Weissmuller said yesterday, "I won't give him his freedom unless he supports the children and me."

Dad had just about had it by this time. He agreed. The divorce proceedings, which had started back in 1943, were concluded in 1948.

Uncle Gordon

No discussion of my parents' divorce would be complete without mention of my uncle Gordon, for he most definitely had a hand in it. He was my mother's brother, some ten years older than she, and he arranged her life for her. Mother would never have dreamed of making a move without first consulting Gordon.

As a young boy, I discovered that Uncle Gordon was gay. He used to take us kids up to the wine country, where he often went to visit his lover, Archie Bianci, whose father owned a big spread up there. By the time I was old enough to realize what gay meant, it had ceased to be important to me. I was brought up in showbiz, where there were so many persons of that persuasion that nobody even talked about it much. No big deal. It still is no big deal to me. What was a big deal, however, were Uncle Gordon's other persuasions, of a more mercenary bent; those quaint attributes impacted upon my father's life and mine.

As I've said, Beryl's father, my Grandpa Scott, owned a business in San Francisco called the Turko-Persian Rug Company, where he worked all of his life. Gordon, who was very much into the art and antique world, worked there also, but only when he had to. He never had much of a business sense, but he did have an uncanny knack for turning a quick buck. He always had some questionable venture going on the side. And, of course, he managed his sister's life. He planned her marriage, planned her estate, planned the children she was to have, and planned—well in advance—her divorce. When Mother announced her intention of marrying Johnny Weissmuller, Gordon told her:

Hollywood marriages seldom work out, Beryl. You'll probably get a divorce within a few years, so plan it well. First, insist upon the most expensive house that your husband can afford. Second, buy the very best antique furnishings and art pieces you can find. Third, if you want to score big, have children, lots of children, right away, one after the other. In almost all divorce settlements, the wife gets the house and furnishings, especially if she has children to support. Fourth, get the very best cash settlement your lawyer can arrange.

I'm not making this up. Mother told me the story herself during one of our many brouhahas later in life. Then she added, "I would never have had you damned kids in the first place if Gordon hadn't insisted!"

*Johnny gets a boost from a bevy of bathing beauties
while impressed locals look on in Blackpool, England.*

*Johnny and Allene take a swimming break while on tour with
the Aquacades in Blackpool shortly after their marriage.*

Be that as it may, all that planning did pay off for her. Gordon saw to it. When, for example, he learned that the taxman was coming over to appraise the house and furnishings, he hurriedly took all the antique furniture out of the house and replaced it with Cost-Plus bamboo pieces. And he used the same strategy with the art—Sears and Roebuck prints replaced the good stuff, which he'd stored in the warehouse of the Turko-Persian Rug Company. Then, as far as Johnny Weissmuller was concerned, the good art and furnishings simply disappeared. I imagine that Beryl shared in the loot somewhere down the line, but, knowing Uncle Gordon as I do, I'm not even sure of that.

I have enough stories about my Uncle Gordon to fill another book, but I don't think I'll tell them here. I will only mention that the old rascal bought an entire city block up on Eddy Street in San Francisco back in the 1950s, and he's still sitting on it, more than forty years later, waiting for the City Revitalization Program to catch up with him. I hope the city does catch up, and I also hope it fines his ass for back taxes. Uncle Gordon must be over ninety now, but he is still as vindictive as ever, so I hear, so I will say no more about him. I'm planning a sequel to this book, which will cover my own Hollywood experiences, and perhaps I can tell the entire Uncle Gordon story there—hopefully when he is dead and less dangerous.

Jungle Jim

As Dad told it,

> Beryl was serious about a divorce this time, and I decided also that it was time. Five years in litigation was enough. So I agreed, divorced your mother, and married Allene—almost in the same breath. I had to get away. I took my new bride to London for a honeymoon—really a working trip for a swimming gig in Blackpool—but I avoided the Claridge. We stayed in a flat overlooking Hyde Park. We walked and talked a lot. I tried to keep it light, but to tell the truth I was worried. I had heavy debts, and I didn't even have a steady job.

But shortly after the honeymooners returned to the States, the cloud above my father's head lifted. Sam Katzman of Columbia Studios, who had put the studio back in the black with his B flicks, heard about Dad's problems and approached him to play Jungle Jim, one of the many comic-strip properties he owned. Together with William Berke, who had begun to specialize in jungle films, Katzman came up with a deal for my father that he couldn't resist. He would be given a say in production, get residuals and a percentage, wear clothes, and speak normally. Dad was delighted! He went on a crash diet, lost thirty-six pounds, and reported for work.

During one of our many talks, I asked my father to tell me about the Jungle Jim experience. He flipped through the pages of one of his scrapbooks and then handed it to me. "It's all in there," he said. "You can read about it. It paid the bills, and I didn't have to work all that hard. It was sort of like having a part-time job that paid more than most full-time jobs. Sam Katzman talked me into it, and the William Morris Agency closed the deal. Columbia Studios filmed it on one of their jungle soundstages. I do remember that I passed my fiftieth birthday while working as Jungle Jim. I also lied a lot. Here, look at this." He pointed to an article by Edith Kermit Roosevelt in the *Los Angeles Daily Times* headed "Erstwhile Tarzan Still Jungle Guy." It read:

> Johnny Weissmuller said today that he is one of the happiest men in the world—he's found a way to make money with almost no work. Johnny, who's starring in a "Jungle Jim" series for Sam Katzman, says he works only a month and a half each year. The rest of the time, he loafs. He throws his leftover salary into real estate, sits back, and lets his business agent do the worrying and make money for him.

Allene recalled those years:

> Your father and I were both very pleased when he got the *Jungle Jim* contract, because he had a percentage of the company—as opposed to the straight salary that he had received

Johnny in an episode of Jungle Jim, *1950.*

from the studios while doing the Tarzan films—and also residuals on replays around the world, as long as he lived. That gave us a better sense of security.

But the security was always tenuous. Everybody assumed that Johnny Weissmuller was a rich man, but when I married him he was already in debt to Bö Roos for some forty thousand dollars. He didn't want to admit this to me, but I wormed it out of him. It was a hole that your father never really dug himself out of. I knew when I married Johnny that there would be financial problems ahead, but I loved that man with all my heart, and I was ready to face those problems, just as long as I could face them with him. I was so proud to be seen with him in public. He was a good dancer and, with a few drinks in him, even a pretty good singer. But what impressed me, and others, the most was the way he dressed.

Allene and Johnny dressed for a night out.

I'm sure that when most people think about Johnny Weissmuller, they visualize him in a bathing suit or a loincloth, but he was always well dressed for public occasions. I think this started when he went to New York to publicize *Tarzan the Ape Man* in 1932. He wore Hollywood casuals, with a turtleneck sweater, and the New York press poked fun at him. After that, he was immaculately dressed in public. During the time he worked for MGM, his entire wardrobe was made by the finest custom tailors in Beverly Hills. His golf clothing was the best and of the finest fabric, and even his golf clubs were custom-made for him. His coif was, of course, impeccably arranged by MGM. He was fastidious and had exquisite taste. He never wore flashy clothing or looked overdressed . . . and your father always put on a good face and tried to present himself to the world as a man without a care, but to tell the truth he was having personal and financial problems long before I married him. He had filed for a divorce against your mother; then she filed separately, and it was very hard for him to get a divorce, and the property settlement thing went on for years—so we were sort of in limbo. After we were able to get married, we started traveling with aquatic-road-show contracts, to make money. For three years, we were constantly on the road during those periods when your father was not making *Jungle Jim* films. It provided good extra money.

We did shows in London and came home for a few months; then we got an offer to go back to England for a couple of months to do another aquatic show. Bö Roos was so pleased with the money coming in that he took us on a tour of Europe (probably on our own money). He took the money for the shows, you see, and gave us an allowance: seventy-five dollars a week for your father, and fifteen dollars a week for me. The rest went against our debt to him.

Around 1950, we got an offer to go to Las Vegas and do a Desert Inn Aquatic Show. That was really good money: $7,500 a week. Not that we saw any of it. Roos merely increased our allowances: one hundred a week for your father, and thirty a week for me. That was it. We were not permitted to gamble or to use any money other than for personal expenses. Roos told the casino managers not to extend us credit. Real high living!

From there, we took our Aquacade on the road throughout the United States. I was never a part of the shows, but I was with your father twenty-four hours a day. We were inseparable, except for the times that I had a golf tournament to play. We had a marvelous time together. Your father was especially happy in those days, despite our money problems. He was doing the two things he loved best—swimming in the aquatic shows and working with animals in *Jungle Jim*. Your father's love of animals was one of the things that made him so endearing to me. All animals, that is, except parrots.

I had heard the story about poor Gary the parrot, and the unfortunate incident that ignited the final bomb in Johnny's marriage to Lupe Vélez, so I was very hesitant about accepting the gift of a parrot named Rags from a friend whose husband was offended by the parrot's language. The bird had been raised by a black family from New Orleans, and they had taught him to swear. He swore profusely, and always in black jargon. My friend's husband told her to get rid of it or he was going to kill it, and I couldn't let that happen, so I took in Rags.

When Johnny came home and saw Rags for the first time, he wasn't pleased, and he asked me what the hell that damned bird was doing in our house. I told him that Rags was just visiting for a few days.

The following week, Johnny asked me again why the bird was still here, and I said, "Rags is just visiting for a few weeks or so." He looked long and hard at the bird, then at me and said, "A few weeks? I thought you said a few days!" I just smiled and said, "He's such a sweet bird, and he doesn't have anyplace else to go. It's just a few weeks or so, can't we keep him?"

Of course, he gave in and let me keep him for a while longer, but a month or so later he asked me again about the

Program cover for the Watercade of 1950.

bird. By then, I was very attached to Rags and just couldn't imagine giving him up. I said, "I've changed my mind. Rags is staying. I just can't take him back. It's Rags or me, Johnny! Take your choice!"

Well, I expected your father to agree right away to that ultimatum, but believe it or not he stared into my eyes for an agonizing thirty seconds—it seemed like an eternity to me—took a long, scowling look at Rags, then shook his head and started laughing. Rags became family.

The bird was hilarious. Every time he heard your father coming up the stairs from the garage, he screamed at the top of his lungs, "God damn bad boy! God damn sumbitch!" But the minute your father entered the room, Rags always cooed, sotto voce, "Hello, my boy!"

Fame and Storm Clouds

The year 1950 was a memorable one for my father and Allene. It kicked off in February, when Johnny Weissmuller was named by the Associated Press and the nation's sportswriters and broadcasters, by a margin of 132 to 102, the "Greatest Swimmer of the Past Fifty Years."

On March 8, 1950, Dad was given a testimonial dinner, sponsored by the Helms Athletic Foundation. Leo Carillo was the master of ceremonies, and the event was attended by champions in various fields. According to the *California Country Club Tee Tattler*,

> Among the special guests invited to pay tribute to the great athlete [Weissmuller] are the following:
> **BASEBALL:** Leo Durocher, Bob Feller, Ralph Kiner, Gus Zernial, Paul Pettit . . . Frank Frisch, and Fred Haney.
> **FOOTBALL:** Bob Waterfield, Jeff Gravath, Red Sanders, and Clark Shaughnessy.
> **BOXING:** Jack Dempsey and Jimmy McLarnin.
> **RACING:** Eddie Arcaro, Jackie Westrope, and Johnny Longden.
> **GOLF:** Ben Hogan, Joe Novak, and Ellsworth Vines.

*Johnny with Bill Shroder, Director of the
Helm's Hall of Fame Foundation, 1950.*

TRACK: Mel Patton and Dean Cromwell.
RADIO: Sam Balter, Sid Ziff, Tommy Harmon . . . Bob
Kelley . . .
Other notables present were Charles Coburn, Stubby Kruger,
Tom Harmon, Forrest Tucker, Buster Crabbe, Johnny's finan-
cial manager, Bö Roos, and Nat Pendleton.

That night, my father was presented with a gold watch, which
was engraved "To Johnny Weissmuller, World's Greatest Swimmer,
1900–1950. From his friends, March 8, 1950." This gold watch
was one of Dad's most prized possessions. As I said earlier, he valued
his movie fame far less than his athletic fame. He had good reason.
His aquatic accomplishments and awards include the following:

- Established sixty-seven world swimming records
- Won fifty-two national swimming championships
- Earned five Olympic gold medals
- Won the Chicago Marathon twice
- Was voted the greatest swimmer of the first half of the century
- Was awarded the Helm's Hall of Fame medal three times
- Was founding chairman of the International Swimming Hall of Fame, Fort Lauderdale, Florida
- Received the Sportsmen's World Award for Swimming in 1968
- Received the American Patriot Award in 1971
- Was awarded special sterling silver Olympic medals at the 1972 Olympic Games in Munich
- Was declared Sportsworld King in 1972
- Received the Dewars Merit Award for Sports Immortal in 1972
- Was declared an undefeated King of Swimming by the International Palace of Sports in 1974
- Was inducted into the American Olympic Hall of Fame in 1983

In April 1950, the citizens of Windber, Pennsylvania, invited my father to a welcome-home celebration held in his honor. The high school's marching band led a motorcade down Main Street (the schools were closed for the event), while Windber's most famous native waved to the crowds from an open car. Local and state newspapers reported the visit in detail, publishing photographs of Dad pointing to the homestead where he claimed to have been born and identifying his brother's baptismal and birth records as his own. According to the *Johnstown Democrat,* "Rev. Father Mackowiak, pastor of the church, presented Johnny with his birth and baptismal certificates and a Miraculous Medal as a gift from the parish. . . ."

The birth certificate was titled "Delayed Certificate of Birth for Petrus John Weissmuller." That, and the baptismal certificate in the same name, were duly witnessed by Grandmother Elizabeth, family

*Falsified, delayed birth certificate of Johny Sr.
showing Windber, PA, as his place of birth.*

members, and various church officials. The deed was now legally done. The delayed certificate of birth shows my father's date and place of birth as June 6, 1905, in Windber, Pennsylvania. To this day, the official Pennsylvania Web site lists Johnny Weissmuller as a native-born son.

I wonder how Windber's city fathers would have tried to explain away the fact that the infant Johnny Weissmuller, who left the City of Rotterdam on January 14, 1905, aboard the *S.S. Rotterdam*, had not, according to their records, even been born yet. But none of that came to light, and the day proceeded without embarrassing historical revelations.

Speaking to the people of Windber, who stood in awe of their visitor in a light spring rain, my father announced, "I have always wanted to see my hometown again, and now I have. This is the biggest thrill I've ever had in my life, and [that includes] my Olympic titles in 1924 and 1928."

Dad carried a stack of cards with him nearly everywhere he went throughout most of his life. He signed them at the request of autograph seekers (the card has been revised and reprinted since his death). On one side was a dramatic photograph of "Tarzan" with the five-circle Olympic emblem. On the other side was a résumé of his swimming credits, concluding with this short sentence: "Throughout his many years, Johnny Weissmuller has traveled to all parts of the world representing so proudly his beloved country, the United States of America."

And it was his beloved country. I don't think I've ever known a man as patriotic as Johnny Weissmuller.

After I had been reunited with my father and was old enough to accompany him, I spent every possible moment with him, not only on film sites and sets, but also at his home. I quickly overcame my initial dislike for Allene, and we became buddies. I perceived early on that Dad and Allene were not happy on the Hollywood circuit. They would rather spend time alone together on the golf course (she was an amateur champion, but Dad was no slouch either), or in the countryside on picnics, or doing almost anything other than joining the constant round of Hollywood parties. Allene and I once talked about this at length. She said,

> We were not really Hollywood people. Perhaps I held your father back a bit, because I was afraid of those damnable parties. Maybe that was because of my own inferiority complex. I only knew that I did not belong with those people. Perhaps this was not good for your father's career, but I really wanted no part of it. It scared me. Too many people that I knew of in that world were hurt badly. Hollywood people were not, as a rule, good people.
>
> As an example of what I'm talking about, I want to tell you a story about my least-favorite Hollywood person of all: Mister Bing Crosby. It was sometime in 1950. We were in bed. The phone rang. It was Bing Crosby. He said, "John, I know it's late, but would you please come up to San Francisco on tonight's train? We're having a benefit golf tournament here

On the set of the Jungle Jim *series in 1953, from left to right:*
Heidi, Johnny Sr., Johnny Jr., Wendy, and Allene.

tomorrow for Benny Coltrin. He just passed away, and he left a wife and two children. We want to raise money for his family, and we need some good Hollywood names to draw the crowds. Dennis Morgan will be here, along with a lot more of Benny's friends and golfing buddies, and we need you to be with us. Okay?"

Of course your father agreed without hesitation. He had known Bing for years and still played golf with him often. I had never met the man, but to me he personified the last shred of dignity and decency left in Hollywood. I would have walked over hot coals for the chance to meet him.

Bing met us at the train station in Glendale the following morning, and we rode with him to San Francisco. I was so excited that I could hardly talk to him. People instantly

At the Bing Crosby Clambake in Pebble Beach:
1952 U.S. Open champion Jim Farrier, Forrest Tucker, Johnny,
and his golf pro, Dave Douglas.

recognized Tarzan, of course, and they crowded around him, begging for autographs. Your father asked me to take Bing's arm and walk on down the concourse, as he wanted to sign a few autographs, and he would join us shortly.

So I took Bing's arm, and we walked through the crowd. People tried to talk with him, but he completely ignored them and stalked onward. Finally, a small boy—who appeared to me mentally retarded—stood directly in our path and held up a small notebook. He stuttered, "Please, Mr. Crosby, would you sign my book for me?" My Hollywood idol, Bing Crosby, looked down at this pathetic little child and said, "Son, why don't you go buy yourself a real book? It might perhaps improve your mind."

He then actually shoved this little boy aside and marched on down the concourse. I don't think that I've ever been so embarrassed or shocked in my entire life! That was the moment that I realized, once and for all, that Hollywood is Hollywood, and everybody associated with it—with the exception of my dear husband—was an absolute phony. I disengaged my arm from that of Mister Bing Crosby and walked on alone. This man may have been an idol to his public, but in private, at least in my view, he was an absolute ass, an insufferable human being.

My father pretty much agreed with Allene about Crosby. They had known each other for years, meeting mostly on the golf course at Lakeside, but Dad said that Bing's behavior there got so bad that nobody really wanted to play with him. He insisted that everyone remain absolutely silent when he approached the ball; nobody was permitted to stand behind him or alongside him; he never wanted to take a break at the third hole for a beer with the other players. Dad said that Crosby was never part of the "in" group. He was so intense about his game—even though he was a horrible 12–15 handicapper—that he began to have trouble finding a foursome.

It got so bad that Bing Crosby decided to start his own tournament. He called it the Clambake, and the first one was held in Arizona. The second was at Pebble Beach on the Monterey Peninsula, and that is where Bing's golf tournament remained. It became a big-time event with the introduction of the Pro-Am feature, and everyone wanted to be seen at it. Beryl Scott was one of the social hostesses who helped promote the Clambake; in fact, that's where she first met Johnny Weissmuller. Eventually, the tournament came to be called, simply, "the Crosby," and Bing—although he remained as boorish as ever—finally had all the golfing partners he could handle.

Allene said that Bing Crosby wasn't the only surprise ass that she discovered in Hollywood; they were legion. A case in point was Red Skelton.

Johnny and Allene with Red Skelton.

"Oh yes," said Allene, "we can't forget dear, funny Red Skelton. We were with Red and his wife at their home one night, and he suggested to Johnny that they switch wives. Big John had me out of that place at warp speed." Allene added that "the only kind of swinging that Tarzan did was on tree vines. Johnny was shocked and humiliated, and after that he was never again friendly with Red Skelton. God, how I learned to hate those people! Perhaps the only innocent working in Tinsel Land at that time was my big, bumbling, trusting Tarzan."

Carolyn Roos Olsen commented recently about Red Skelton:

It was always assumed that I would work with Dad [Bö Roos] in his business, and after attending business college and majoring in accounting, that's what I did, at the age of nineteen. One of the first persons I met in Dad's office was Red Skelton. He was a charming man, and we quickly became enamored of each other. His wife, Edna, approved. Theirs was a strange relationship. Red never drank in those days, and he was always chewing on a huge cigar. He was like a big kid. He called Edna "Mommy," and she treated him like a son. When I got married at age twenty-one and took off, Red cried. I think his wife did too. I actually accompanied them once on a trip to New York, and I watched while Edna ushered an old girlfriend out the back door while a new girlfriend was coming in the front door.

Georgia [whom Red later married] was also crazy in sexual matters. She and Red would often call up an agency and order in two girls, one for each. Stuff like that. Red started drinking while living with Georgia. Eventually, he slowed down and started painting clowns. I still have two of his original clown paintings. Charming guy . . . strange guy. . . .

Bing Crosby sneering at crippled children and pushing them around? So offensive and ill mannered on the golf course that nobody wanted to play with him? And Red Skelton a sex maniac? Are there no sacred Hollywood icons left to us?

Getch

After my father and mother were divorced, Beryl married a couple more times. The first of these marriages was to Robert Henry Ginter, also known as "Getch." A big German lunk who came on as a Nazi bully, Getch was working for the Bell Tone hearing-aid company when he and my mother met at a Santa Monica swimming club; she was there playing bridge. He hustled her, married her, stole what was left of the Weissmuller money, and used it to start a personal management agency in partnership with a guy named Paul Serf. He even moved Serf into an upstairs bedroom in the east wing of our house (it was a huge place), where he remained until he died, a short while later, of a heart attack.

Getch then became the sole owner of the agency, and he went on to represent a great many celebrities and show people. I remember that he tried to woo Rock Hudson into his stable. Rock didn't become a client, but he did become a wonderful family friend. He was a gentle, kindly soul, and I was deeply saddened by his tragic death.

Getch amassed quite a fortune, and he and my mother spent it lavishly. I certainly can't list poverty and deprivation among my childhood woes. Getch did not like children, however, and he ran the family like a tyrant. I didn't like Getch, and I rebelled so strongly that after our first few squabbles he ignored me completely. As far as he was concerned, I was on my own. Getch and my mother then took off on world cruises, or whatever, unencumbered by children.

My sisters and I stayed home with Nursie and scrounged for food in the refrigerator. We had fine clothes and went to the best schools, but my mother's idea of a balanced diet for children consisted of chopped-olive sandwiches and peanut butter. I often got so hungry that I would wait for the Helm's bread truck and snag doughnuts and sweet rolls.

Nursie was something of a Nazi herself. She broke coat hangers across my back and constantly beat on Heidi. Wendy escaped most of this, but only because she had a club foot. I hated Getch, and I grew to dislike my mother intensely. I spent as little time at home as I could possibly manage. The only bright spot during that period of my life was when Granny Scott (Beryl's mother) came for a visit and caught Nursie stealing my mother's nylons. Nursie was fired on the spot. Granny Scott was almost as tough a lady as my mother was.

Robert Henry Ginter eventually died a rich man, but none of us, including my mother, ever saw much of his fortune. Most of it went to his children from an earlier marriage, who lived in Oxnard, California. Getch never liked me as a kid, and he liked me even less as a grown man. Once, in front of Diane, I told him what a miserable, rotten, selfish, arrogant, unfeeling sonofabitch I thought he was. I wasn't too surprised that he didn't leave me a penny. He did leave me memories, however, and one of the most hateful was of Harvard Military Academy. Getch shipped me there during my second year in junior high school; at the same time, he shipped my sisters off to a Swiss boarding school. He wanted us out of the way so that he could travel freely with Beryl.

Naughty Boys

I entered Harvard Military Academy with Jimmy Mitchum, Bob Mitchum's son. We were both rowdies in those days—I imagine that Big Bob shipped Jimmy there just to get him out of his hair.

I got into trouble almost from the first day. I hated the place. I was sitting in a history class one day not paying much attention, and the teacher noticed me. He was a big guy who also just happened to be the football coach, and he came over to my desk and whacked me with a book. He hit me so hard that he cut me across the eye, and I threw up all over him. He was amazed—and so was my mother—because I was not a delicate kid. I never got sick. Mother called in a doctor, who checked me out and said that I had a ruptured appendix. This would lead to my first meeting with Dad since I was three and a half years old.

I remember that the doctor's name was Platt. Dr. Platt informed my mother that my appendix had burst out of its sac and then grown around my back. My condition was serious, and he recommended that my mother call my father and any other close relatives. In fact, because my life was threatened, my mother was obliged by law to notify my father. She did so grudgingly; I have known few people who could hate as long and as passionately as my mother.

So Dad came to visit me in the hospital. Unfortunately, he brought Allene with him. The look on Mother's face could have ignited a fire. Dad gave me a small balsa-wood airplane, and I tossed it into the air. The damned thing sailed right out the window. There was an embarrassed silence, and then everyone laughed—nervously.

Allene was a gorgeous woman. I hated her on sight. Keep in mind that at this point in my life, I knew nothing about my mother's infidelities and nothing about her using my sisters and me as bait to try to punish my father. I only knew what she had told me: Dad had other women in his life, and that was why he never came to see me. I believed her—after all, if you can't trust your own mother, whom can you trust? And here, right in front of me, was one of those "other women." Mother had told me all about her: California state golfing champion, whom everyone spoke of as the next Babe Didrickson; *darling* (my mother's tonal emphasis) of the Riviera

Country Club set; and so forth. The hatred in the room was oppressive. My father claimed that I broke through it by asking, "Win any medals lately, Dad?" He laughed and said, "Yeah, a few."

When this difficult reunion was finally over, I was still left with bad feelings about my father. It took too many years, unfortunately, for me to realize just how thoroughly brainwashed I had been as a child.

⌒

After recuperating from my appendix operation, I returned to Harvard. Jimmy Mitchum told me that they had given the teacher who hit me a week off with pay, saying that the man had been under "undue stress." Small wonder, when he had to deal with the likes of Johnny Weissmuller Jr. and Jimmy Mitchum.

Although I didn't like the place, it did have a good swim team. I wasn't supposed to swim on the varsity team until my junior year, but the school waived that restriction, and I went on to break every swimming record that Harvard Military Academy had ever set. I also set some behavioral records outside of school. We had hardly been enrolled—I guess we were still thirteen—when Jimmy Mitchum and I stole a car. It started out as a bad idea and ended up an absolute disaster.

At the Mitchum house, there was a pool table in a room over the garage. Jimmy and I shot pool there one day until we were thoroughly bored, and then we hatched the bright idea of heisting a neighbor's Nash Rambler. We snuck down the back stairs, convinced that no one was watching, and hot-wired the car using the foil from a pack of Marlboro cigarettes. We made it about twelve feet up the road before the foil fell out and the car died. We plugged it back in and moved along another twelve feet or so, and damned if the foil didn't fall out again. By that time, the owner of the car was running behind us, yelling, "Jimmy, John, stop that shit right now!"

I knew he couldn't see us because it was dark, but he'd made a good guess at the identity of the culprits. We were scared, so we jumped into a culvert on the side of the street, crawled up a bank, then ran like hell back down the road to Jimmy's house. We went back up to the poolroom, talking and laughing about our little escapade. Suddenly, Bob Mitchum entered the room. The first words out of his mouth were "You stupid sonsofbitches!"

What we didn't know was that Bob had witnessed the entire operation and had been waiting for us to return. He was a big, strong guy, but he didn't kick our butts, though we richly deserved it. Instead, he gave us a cussing out the likes of which I had never experienced before and have not experienced since: "You miserable little shits! You ignorant little bastards! You wretched, incompetent little . . ." He went on to say things that shock me to this day, and I've spent most of my adult life on the waterfront. Bob Mitchum was a dear friend of mine, but when he was angry he had the most creative vocabulary of any man I've ever known. He ended his tirade with words to this effect: "I don't like thieves, and I especially don't like amateur thieves. You punks couldn't even heist a tricycle without getting caught. I don't recommend stealing, but for Christ's sake, if you're going to boost a car, at least boost a Cadillac!"

I was impressed. I did manage to get into a few more escapades with Jimmy Mitchum, but that lecture certainly influenced both of us to terminate our criminal careers. The rest of the stuff we did could merely be classified as obnoxious behavior.

Bö Christian Roos

My father worked on the *Jungle Jim* series for seven years, from 1948 to 1955. As he mentioned, the money was good, and the working hours were short, and he was confident that he was in a healthy financial condition due to investments carefully managed by his business agent, Bö Roos. "Yeah, good old Bö," Dad said,

> he really took care of me. I don't really remember not having Bö Roos around. I don't recall whether he hired me or I hired him, but he was my business and financial manager ever since the time that I had more than a quarter in my pocket to worry about. And he was much more than my business manager: Bö Roos was my friend. Then Beryl told me that Roos was stealing

from me. I didn't believe her. My friends, including some who had been associated with Bö and had dropped him, also told me that he was stealing from me. I didn't believe them. Bö Roos was my friend. He would never steal from me! I trusted the man completely.

I guess I first woke up and saw the writing on the wall when I began receiving calls from your mother complaining that alimony and child-support checks were not being paid. Hell, I had been averaging at least two thousand dollars a week since the early 1930s. I spent a lot, of course, but it was augmented by interest and the "good investments" that Roos assured me that he was making in my behalf; I still had to be worth at least enough to cover my alimony checks. I called Roos and asked him what was going on. After a few hems and haws, he came to the brutal point: "Johnny, you're broke. I can't make payments on your debts with money that you don't have."

"Broke!" I screamed at him. "What the hell are you talking about? Where did it all go?"

"You spent it all, Johnny. I tried to tell you, but you wouldn't listen to me. It's all your own fault. I wash my hands of the matter!"

I was so angry that I guess I lost it and threatened to kill the man. He sobbed in typical Bö fashion and said, "Johnny, what do you want of me? I have done the best that I could for you! I'm a sick man. First you break my heart, now you want to kill me?"

Yeah, I did want to kill him. But, try as I could, I never, not to this day, got a straight answer from Bö Roos about what happened to my money. I had to face up to the fact that I was, indeed, a poor man once again.

I was in a state of shock. This was the last straw. Allene and I had been having marital problems for some months, and that was only temporarily put on hold when I bought her a four-thousand-dollar sapphire ring with my final *Jungle Jim* paycheck. It had been apparent to me for some time that the

Johnny Sr. relaxing on set.

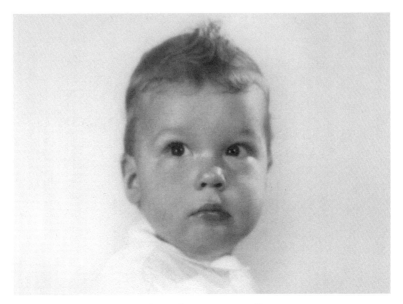

His nibs, Johnny Weissmuller Jr.

Tarzan and son.

From left: Mike Oliver, Allene, Johnny Sr.,
and Johnny Jr. at the Los Flamingos Hotel, 1955.

Johnny Weissmuller Jr.; the one and only son of Tarzan.
From the Paris edition of *Elle*, October 1995.

The on-screen magic of Johnny Sr. and Maureen.

In *Tarzan Finds a Son!*, Tarzan explains what he has
done with the guns he pilfered during the night.

With director Richard Thorpe, Tarzan rests between takes
for *Tarzan's New York Adventure*.

Johnny Sr. and Maureen look at a model
of a headhunter's village for the *Tarzan Finds a Son!* set.

Johnny Sr. swimming on the set in 1936.

Tarzan takes a dive at Earl's Court in 1948.

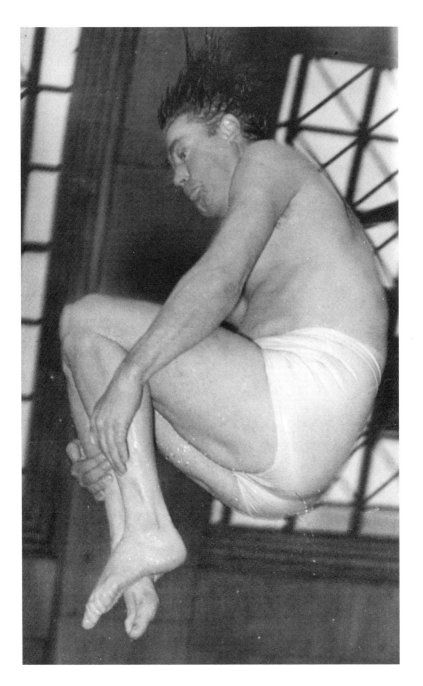

Taking the plunge at Earl's Court.

JOHNNY WEISSMULLER

The illustrious star of the
Jungle Movies and the greatest swimmer
of all times

S. & R. ENTERPRISES INC.

Eastern Office
150 W. 46th Street
New York 19, N. Y.
Lu. 2-5183

Proudly present
In Person
JOHNNY WEISSMULLER
in WATERCADE of 1950

California Office
Culver Hotel
Culver City,
California

STAGED AND PRODUCED BY NOEL SHERMAN

Executive Director	Bo. Chr. Roos
Producer and General Manager	Noel Sherman
Assistant to Noel Sherman on Stage Choreography	Honey Johnson
Assistant to Noel Sherman on Water Sequences	Ann Newcomb
Company Manager	Lincoln Widder
Press Representative	Wilson Heller
Musical Director	Marty Beck
Musical Score and Arrangements	Steve Childs
Costumes by	Mlle. Marie and Variety Costume Co.
Chief Carpenter	Tex Hamilton
Superintendents of Construction	Joe Sabol and Paul Bucknell
Art Construction and Layouts	Harry Hochfeld

Bathing Suits worn by *Aquanymphs* by GANTNER AND MATTERN, San Francisco
Sava-Wave Bathing Caps exclusively worn by *Aquanymphs*, by KLEINERT of New York
Playing dates for Arena Managers Association arranged by Norman Frescott.

NOEL SHERMAN

is an old hand at show business and directing of out-
standing spectacles. It was with him that the idea
of a combined water and stage musical revue
originated and he is the first producer to
successfully create and present a port-
able water and stage musical revue,
here in the United States,
and in England.

A page from the program for the Watercade
of 1950 lists the participants.

Our own movie idol of the jungle films, the movie's long time rugged "TARZAN" and "JUNGLE JIM," is embarking on a personal tour for the first time. Johnny Weissmuller was recently voted officially by an overwhelming majority of the nation's

JOHNNY WEISSMULLER

sportwriters as *greatest swimmer of the half century.* Johnny Weissmuller won five Olympic championships and broke 67 world records, many of which have never been broken, and he remains as the only champion who retired undefeated in his competitive career.

Johnny Sr.'s description in the program for the Watercade.

Reading Tarzan's palm — what does the future hold?

Johnny Sr. and Allene on *The Ed Sullivan Show* in 1950.

At the New York World's Fair. From left: Morton Downey,
Edward G. Robinson, and Johnny Sr.

From left: Johnny Sr., Stan Laurel, Ginny Hopkins
(synchronized swimming champ of the New York World's Fair),
Morton Downey, and Oliver Hardy

Johnny Sr., Allene, and John Wayne.

From left: Nick Petripolo (1950 City Champ, California
Country Club), Red Skelton, and Johnny Sr.

Johnny Weissmuller Sr. is welcomed home
in Windber, Pennsylvania.

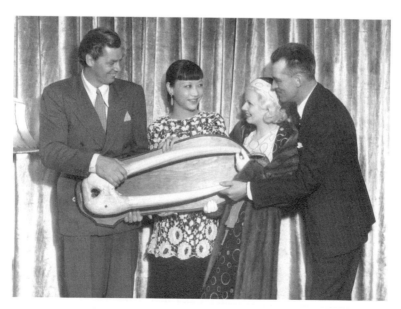

Yet another award for Weissmuller. From left: Johnny Sr.,
Anna Mae Wong, Jean Harlow, and Woody Van Dyke.

Johnny Sr. displays his 1950 Swimmer
of the Half-Century trophy from the Helms Foundation.

Johnny Sr. and Allene leaving for their honeymoon.

difference in our ages was just too great. I loved Allene, but we were growing apart at a fast pace. And now to learn that I was almost dead broke? It was almost too much to contemplate.

I thought about it for a while; then I heard myself mumbling, "Tarzan work now!" That sounded funny, so I started mumbling more great lines, such as "Tarzan hungry!"; "Tarzan need gold!"; "Tarzan buy food!"; "Tarzan steal white man gold!"; "Umgawa! Tarzan think good!" I smiled, then giggled, then broke out in laughter so hard that tears ran down my cheeks. When it was all over, I did feel a lot better. It had been a long time since I had found anything to laugh about. Maybe it was time to learn how again. I picked up the phone and began to call friends. I didn't beat about the bush. I told them that I was broke and needed a job.

The response was immediate but guarded and low-key. What kind of a job does one offer an ex-king?

Allene recalled those near-broke days as the beginning of the end of their marriage. She also told me that the ring that Dad gave her was a cornflower-blue star sapphire, larger even than Lana Turner's. He'd bought it from a golf-course pawnbroker with earnings from a Desert Inn Aquacade show, not with his last *Jungle Jim* paycheck. In addition, he'd paid two thousand dollars for it, not four thousand. Allene almost lost it while standing at the rail of a cruise ship some twenty years ago. The stone dropped out, but luckily it fell into her hand instead of the water. She took the ring to a jeweler to have it repaired, and the jeweler appraised the stone at eighty thousand dollars. Allene remarked, "Eighty thousand dollars sounds great now, but where was the value when we really needed it?"

Allene offered me her own recollections of Bö Roos:

I guess the beginning of the end of our marriage centered on Bö Roos. Was he a crook? Well, we were never able to prove it, but I think the evidence of that might be inferred from the fact that so many of his clients left him, with hard feelings. These were board members in a company, owned by Bö, called the Beverly Management Corporation. None of them ever tried to prosecute Roos, because, as various members of that group told me, Bö told them all that there had been questionable tax practices with this corporation, and if they tried to take him down, he would take the rest of the board members down with him.

Roos ran his business with an iron fist. He would, for example, loan money, at considerable interest, to clients, such as us, who occasionally needed an advance. We couldn't just sign for everything. It was always easy to get extra money, even large sums of money, from Roos, but to do so we had to sign notes secured by our home. One day I said, "Johnny, I'm not going to sign these notes any longer!" Your father insisted, "You must sign them, Allene. We need the money!"

As I told you, when I married your father, he was already in debt to Roos to the tune of some forty thousand dollars, and we eventually owed him a great deal more than that. And there were debts other than those owed to Roos that nagged us constantly. Tax write-offs were our worst problem. We got into so much trouble with the IRS over tax write-offs that were not permissible that we also owed them more than we could ever hope to pay. Johnny often told me that Bö Roos always gave his clients good tips on tax write-offs. Some tips. We discovered that most of our write-offs were not considered legal by the IRS. With a good business manager, that problem should never have arisen.

Johnny and I had a house, which we had built in 1952, on Lorenzo Street in Cheviot Hills, near where my parents lived. It was a lovely home, and your father and I put our initials in the cement of the driveway before moving in. We lived in it together, happily, until 1961, when we had our first separation. That same year, Bö Roos (at the insistence of another board

*Johnny displays his golf trophies in his "Championship Corner"
at the Lorenzo Street house, 1955.*

member, named Fred MacMurray) evicted me and took the house, which was the collateral for all those loans.

It was a terrible time in my life. Johnny was by this time living with María [who would become his fifth wife], and Bö, controlling all the money, had not been paying my bills. He did not pay the gardener, and the gardener attached my car for back-salary payments. He had not paid the electric or water bills, and those utilities were cut off. I had to go to my mother's house to take a shower and wash my hair. And then the eviction from my own house! I was so upset by all this that I carelessly fell down while leaving the premises and broke my leg. While recovering at a friend's home, I received a large bouquet of flowers from Bö, with a note of condolence for my accident. He was something else.

It would be an understatement to say that Bö Roos was a unique individual. He was Mister Personality. Ostensibly kind and gentle, he never raised his voice, and everybody who met him instantly trusted him. He was, for sure, in the right job.

But not everybody was taken in by Roos. The wife of Frank Borzage, Nita, was a pretty smart little girl. She worked at the California Country Club, in the office. She got Frank away from Bö right away. She said to Frank, "This man is stealing from you. He is taking your money. You don't need him." Thanks to Nita, Frank was one of the lucky ones.

Your mother never liked or trusted Roos. She never went along with the complete trust that your father had in this man. That was one of the reasons for the great bitterness in their divorce. Beryl told me that Bö was stealing them blind, and Johnny wouldn't listen to her. She said that her first "proof" that this was happening was when she discovered substantial dry-cleaning charges for suits that Johnny Weissmuller did not own. Upon inquiring at the cleaner's, she was told that the suits in question belonged to Mr. Roos. Beryl was afraid that if Roos was stealing on a small scale, then he also might well be stealing on a larger scale in areas almost impossible to locate and document. She smelled big troubles ahead and just wanted out of the whole thing.

My own father tried to tell Johnny about Roos, but he wouldn't listen to him. I remember his reply was "Bö wouldn't do that to me! He's my friend!" Your father trusted Bö completely.

As she recalled this period of her life, Allene wiped away a tear. She said that after she and Dad were separated in 1961, she hired a divorce lawyer. Then she added,

Shortly afterwards, your father also hired the same attorney—crazy as it sounds to have people in a divorce action using the same lawyer—but it was a very amicable, civilized separation and divorce. The lawyer also looked into the charges that Bö Roos was stealing from us and, if so, whether anything could be recovered. Nothing could be proven.

Keep in mind that all of the money that your father made from his work went directly to Roos. When we wanted money, we had to ask Bö for it. He was in complete charge of anything and everything having to do with money. When we wanted to buy anything above our weekly allowance, we had to ask Roos for the money. He would always advance it, but only against our home as collateral, and we both had to sign the notes. . . . This is so difficult for me to talk about. I don't want any trouble or to cause embarrassment to the remaining family of Bö Roos. His son and daughter are still living. It is so difficult because everything is really just suspect. We were never able to actually prove any wrongdoing on the part of Bö.

Carolyn Roos Olsen had the following to say about the controversy surrounding her father in a recent interview:

I suppose that the people who knew my father, and especially those who worked with him, or for him, called him good or bad depending upon whether he was helping them or hindering them. The big stars in his stable (and he had some of the biggest names in the business) liked to be helped—in fact, they liked to be coddled, but they didn't like to be told by their business manager that they were spending more than they were making. When the big bucks were coming in, and all the bills were being paid, and there was even money left over for investments for the future, my father was a "good" business manager. When more money started going out than was coming in, and Dad told them to cool it, sometimes even putting them on strict budgets, he was a "bad" business manager.

My father maintained close relationships with all of his clients—sometimes, I think, too close. Managing a stable of superegos was no easy task, and often the lines between friendship and business became blurred. I think this may have happened in the case of Johnny Weissmuller. I never heard about any problems between Johnny and my father. To the contrary. They were about the same age, both acted like big, overgrown kids, and they partied and played together constantly. I remember, for example, that Dad and Johnny used to go up to the top floors of hotels in San Francisco and make a waterfall down the stairs with a fire hose. Once, in Dad's convertible, with Cesar Romero, they drove across the Bay Bridge—in reverse.

If my father had one fault as a business manager, it was this tendency he had to become too close to his clients. Sometimes I thought he needed a business manager himself. He was quite the playboy. The girls were always there. I remember he had a beach house in Malibu that he never told my mother about (even though she knew that he had it). It was his little hideaway, and he went there often with his friends and clients. I recall Victor Mature running around down there with these little Peruvian gals. All kinds of kinky stuff happened in the Malibu hideaway. It's the old, old story about what happens to people who have an ego that needs to be fed.

But concerning Johnny Weissmuller, the biggest problem, if there was one, as I see it, was the fact that Johnny and Allene just kept on spending money and wanting more. And it simply wasn't there. I think Dad just got tired of loaning them money all the time and knowing that he wasn't going to get it back. I think it was just as simple as that. Just a money problem. These stars, and their wives, simply didn't understand. They would look at the money coming in, but they wouldn't see where it was going out. They had agents to pay, mortgages to pay, servants to pay, yet all they wanted to do was go out and have a good time. A lot of people have money problems, but it's only when they have a big name that you hear about it. Then it becomes big news. Their friends tell them, "After you made him so much money, he's not going to carry you for the next ten years? Oh, how terrible!"

I remember that Dad tried and tried to keep Weissmuller from spending so much. He carried him for years, loaning him money. I found lots of notes in Dad's files, signed by Johnny Weissmuller, which were never paid back. Johnny had a hell of a bad time with the money problems. It occurs to me that a lot of these women you may have talked to about Bö Roos don't know peas from potatoes about what went on in his business. Like, they may have wound up losing their homes because they, or their husbands, spent too much money. Whose fault was that? For sure, my father was a very tough business-man, and if he had to occasionally foreclose on properties to get his money back, that, to him, was simply business—cer-tainly not theft or fraud. . . .

After saying all these things, I want to emphasize that I have always liked and admired Allene so much. She is such a sweet person, and to this day I consider her my friend. We may have differing opinions about my father, but we are all entitled to our own opinions. As far as I'm concerned, this controversy does not in any way affect our friendship. To my mind, this is a monumental misunderstanding. I must call Allene and talk to her about this. . . .

I am sure that this was a most difficult time for my father, and it became a painful memory for Allene. Was Allene right about Bö? In all fairness to Roos, I must say that Dad was somewhat irrespon-sible with money, and for years Bö had been telling him to slow down. Johnny Weissmuller never took advice from anybody. He made his own decisions. I suppose there are always two sides to every story, and I remember well both Dad and Beryl talking about the heyday of the Hollywood Rat Pack, when they lived high on the hog and enjoyed the best of everything—all paid for by Roos, against my father's earnings. Signing bills is convenient, but the day of reckoning always comes. As I see it, Dad and Beryl dug the financial hole; Allene fell into it and never really managed to climb out.

I once asked Dad how he could have continued to sign all those notes to Roos when he must have known that he was running up monumental debts. He replied, "I guess I can blame Big Bill

Bachrach. Every piece of paper he ever put before me I signed without looking at it. I was conditioned to trust and obey. So every piece of paper that Roos ever put before me I also signed, without looking at it. Dumb? I guess. But that's what happened. Unknowingly, I signed away a fortune."

As much as I loved my father, I have to admit that he was in many ways a vacillator. He hated to make hard decisions. He was brave and strong—in fact, he was almost foolishly fearless—in physical confrontations, but when it came to life confrontations, those involving family and business responsibilities, he would waver. He could never say no. And when his perception of things went awry, he tended to blame others rather than himself. I cannot help but believe that Dad knew exactly what he was doing when he signed those little bits of paper that Bö shoved in front of him. I am not saying that I believe that Roos was Mister Clean, but a lot of Dad's financial problems he brought upon himself. Fair is fair.

I have heard so many different stories and descriptions of Bö Roos over the years that I am confused myself. Mike Oliver, for example, swears that Roos was nothing but a good and faithful friend and manager to Johnny Weissmuller, as well as to the other stars in his stable. I suppose the truth will never be known in its entirety, but the fact remains that my father was in very poor financial condition when his relationship with Roos finally ended.

Hollywood Orphan

Dad was a poor man not only because of Roos, but also because my mother got quite a large cash settlement from the divorce for maintenance and child support. Because of that cash settlement, our lifestyle did not diminish appreciably. I was talking with my father's other "Boy" recently, Johnny Sheffield, and it occurred to me that we had grown up in the same kind of world. He went to studio schools with the likes of Mickey Rooney and Judy Garland; I was surrounded by movie stars and their children.

During my high school years, for example, my best friend was Patrick "Ryan" O'Neal. Pat and I also started acting at about the same time. In 1957, through his father, Blackie, Pat got a part in a short-lived TV series called *The Viking*. At about the same time, I won a role in MGM's *Andy Hardy Comes Home,* with Mickey Rooney. Jimmy Mitchum was working during this period in the film *Thunder Road,* and Burt Reynolds had the part of the blacksmith in the TV series *Gunsmoke*. We were all part of that amorphous group of young, aspiring actors who would hang around the studio casting lots looking for film work through the "cattle call" system. That's how casting directors and producers hunt for talent to fill roles that are undefined; they go to cattle calls in search of someone who "looks" the part.

It was through my association with this group of young actors that I got involved in the Hollywood Football League. Some of the league members were stuntmen, some were ex-football players, and all were in very good physical condition. Burt had played college ball in Florida, and he'd once considered turning pro. It was his idea to start a team to compete with the teams of Ricky Nelson and Elvis Presley, which played every Saturday afternoon at a junior-college field down in the San Fernando Valley.

One rule of the Hollywood Football League was made very clear: no hitting in the face. Every person in the league assumed that he would soon be playing the lead role in a film; facial disfigurement would not be tolerated. So we played flag football. Each player attached a flag to his body, and if an opposing player snatched the flag away, that was a tackle.

This system worked well until first Burt, and then Ricky and Elvis, started bringing in "redshirt" ringers. Redshirts were players who worked out with college or even professional teams, such as the L.A. Rams. Nobody knew who they were, but they sure as hell weren't amateurs. After that, the games simply got too rough. Redshirts didn't give a damn about rules such as no hitting in the face. One would grab your flag, and another would pile into you offside at a hundred miles an hour. After a few players had sustained serious sprains and bruises, the Hollywood Football League was dissolved. It only lasted about six months, but all involved decided that it was long enough. We had acting careers to pursue.

William Randolph Hearst and my father were lifelong friends, and the Hearst mansion in San Simeon was like a second home to me— albeit a home somewhat larger than any other I'd ever been in. Hearst installed a lovely mosaic swimming pool there, and, with my father's Olympic triumphs in mind, Hearst said to him during a visit, "Hey, Johnny, why don't you try out my new pool?" Dad did so, then said, jokingly, "It's a beautiful pool for sure, Bill, but much too short for me. If it wasn't for the fact that I swim with my head out of water, I'd probably bump my noggin at the far end before I even got in stride!"

The following week, Hearst ripped out that beautiful pool and installed a new one (also mosaic-tiled) of Olympic size.

Joan Crawford was our neighbor, and I spent a lot of time in her home. I am saddened to hear and read unflattering stories about her. I remember Joan as a dear lady who bounced me on her knee when I was a toddler and was very kind to me, even through my wild teen years. Yet I understand how stories such as *Mommie Dearest* can surface in that convoluted community of stars and children of stars. Don Gallery, actor, writer, and Hollywood historian (now retired, living in Puerto Vallarta, and serving as president of the Vallarta Writers Group), shares my impressions:

> I grew up on Rockingham, in Brentwood, near the Weissmuller and Crawford homes. My mother was a well-known actress named ZaSu Pitts. I remember Joan Crawford as a charming, soft-spoken lady. No more, no less. I think that children of famous Hollywood parents often protest too much. They never remember when their parents took them to the zoo or the circus and bought them ice-cream cones, or caressed them and read stories to them and told them how much they loved them. They only remember the bad things, like being alone when their parents were responding to the demands of their own Hollywood masters. Perhaps this selective lapse of memory has something to do with the fact that salacious stories sell more books than those of a more innocuous genre. . . .

My godmother was Jean Harlow. Louis B. Mayer of MGM Studios was "Uncle Louie." Probably fifty of the big-name stars in Hollywood knew who my mother and godmother and Uncle Louie were, and they knew the names of the other brats of Hollywood stars. And so did every good businessman from Malibu to Brentwood. We kids never carried money. We didn't even know what money was. We got ten dollars a month in pocket change for ice cream and candy and other minor expenses, and that was it. But we could go into any store, just about anywhere in California, and sign for any damned thing we wanted. And the bill got paid. How? By whom? Bö Roos? Uncle Louis? Who cared? The only people who really knew how the game was played were the merchants; and they smiled all the way to the bank.

Don is right that we Hollywood brats were different from other people, and we knew it. Never mind that my father and mother were divorced, I was still the son of Tarzan, and things changed very little for me and for my mother. We were part of the *community*. Even though we kids were often abandoned by one or the other of our parents, sacrificed to their quest for fame or social stature, we were never really abandoned by the community of the Hollywood elite. They were our family. They would protect their own.

The members of this elite were, however, typically a bit eccentric, and they frequently took their wealth for granted. Many passed this attitude on to their children—the Hollywood brats. One of those brats was the daughter of Marion Davies. The former silent and talkie comedienne and movie star of the 1920s and 1930s, as well as philanthropist and loving companion of William Randolph Hearst for thirty years, had at one time pawned her jewelry to help Hearst when he was in financial trouble. The jewelry was worth millions of dollars. Marion Davies didn't buy at Woolworths. I will never forget seeing one of her brooches. It was shaped like an unfurled American flag and set with huge red, white, and blue rubies, diamonds, and sapphires. The forty-eight stars were diamonds, of course. I have seen pictures of a magnificent red, white, and blue ruby-diamond-sapphire ring owned by Charlotte Maillard Shultz (wife of former Secretary of State George Shultz), but the Marion Davies brooch made the Shultz ring look like Cracker Jack loot.

The Davies jewelry was later redeemed from the pawnshop, and, upon her death, Marion willed it to her daughter, Patty (Hearst) Lake. Some time later, Arthur Lake Sr. (who played Dagwood in the *Blondie* series), his son, A.P. (Artie) Lake, Patty, and I picked up this jewelry, which was stored in a cigar box, from an estate lawyer in Santa Monica and headed back to the Lake home in Palm Springs.

En route, we stopped at a little gas station in Ojai, and Patty went into the restroom, taking the cigar box with her. She left the jewelry there, on the bathroom counter. It was not until we arrived in Palm Springs that we discovered the loss, and we raced like bats out of hell back to the gas station.

An old man was sweeping the place. Responding to our desperate queries, he told us that, sure, he had found a cigar box full of old, worthless geegaws in the bathroom. He'd stuck it somewhere in the storeroom, and he went to fetch it. The man almost had a stroke when we told him what those "geegaws" were worth.

The Hollywood brats with whom I hung out while I was growing up had almost no concept of the value of money—or of the value of anything else, come to think about it. I discovered early on that most famous people are not much brighter than the rest of us. They just have more money to throw away.

I think my Hollywood friends looked on me as a kind of neglected orphan. They went out of their way to befriend poor "Little John." I really don't know why, because most of them were also products of broken homes—it was almost the norm. At any rate, Julie London and Bobby Troup arranged therapeutic bongo lessons for me, and I became pretty good on them. I once played bongos with James Dean. What I remember best about Julie was her losing her swimsuit top in the pool. I will decline to elaborate on that story.

Red Skelton was one of our next-door neighbors, and he was a fine neighbor to have. During a big fire in Bel-Air, when houses all around ours were in danger of burning and our neighbors were out in their yards with their hoses, spraying their houses with water, Red saved our house and many others by calling in his personal fire department from Skelton Studios. Imagine having your own fire department!

Andre Previn lived some distance away, but this fire was a big one, and soon his house was also in danger. I was Previn's gofer (go for this, go for that)—he hired me to do odd jobs for him all the time. He began to depend upon me, I suppose. During the fire, he phoned and asked me to come over and help him protect his house. When I arrived, Andre was standing next to his car, which was by now totally consumed by flames. His face streaked black, a set of car keys dangling from his soot-covered hand, he looked at me mournfully and asked, "Do you think it will start, John?"

And then there was Beryl. I had been out on the town until three the night before the big fire, and I didn't get out of bed until ten that morning. When I got up, I found my mother and her poodle, Rik, getting set to leave the house. Mom was wearing a sable coat. She had a mink coat under one arm, and she was holding a gin bottle in each hand. All she said to me was "John, the house is on fire." She then marched out to her car and drove off with Rik and her loot and left me standing there with my mouth open. My mother's priorities—what she deemed worth saving—had been well established, and they obviously did not include me.

I decided that if the house was going to burn, I should at least try to save something, so I wrapped the most expensive paintings in wet blankets and threw all the good crystal and silverware into the pool. Then I sprayed the outside of the house with water. Luckily, it did not burn down. When Mother returned home, the incident was scarcely mentioned.

There was only one Beryl.

Johnnys Jr. and Sr. sailfishing in Acapulco, 1955.

During my last year in high school, I moved into the home of my father and Allene. I had gone to Paul Revere Junior High; after that I did the short stint at the Harvard Military Academy; then I attended University High School, because I lived in West Los Angeles, and it was a requirement to attend high school in your district. After moving to my father's house in Cheviot Hills, I enrolled in Hamilton High, from which I eventually graduated. Years later, I attended both UCLA and USC on swimming scholarships. That was a piece of cake for me. I had been coached by the best.

Dad had me in the water training to be an Olympic swimmer at the age of two years. At three and a half, I was just getting the hang of it when that rattrap ended it all. But, during my teen years, after I became free to visit my "coach," we spent a lot of time swimming together. The Old Man said that I was better than he was at the same age. Flattering but highly doubtful. Still, he persisted, and he also persuaded his erstwhile swimming and clown-diving buddy, Stubby Kruger, to help train me. I loved Stubby, and he was a great coach. He agreed with Dad that I was good and could have been a fine competitive swimmer, but he also perceived that my heart wasn't in it; I couldn't commit to the many hard hours of training that it takes to become a real champion. Stubby said I didn't have the hunger. He was right.

The last time I saw Stubby Kruger was around 1958, and he was so bent over and crippled that he tried to avoid me. He was embarrassed about his physical disability. I ran over and grabbed his hand anyway. I didn't know what had caused his physical problems, nor did I care. I respected his disinclination to discuss it. Crippled or not, Stubby Kruger was one of my heroes. I was happy to see him.

It was while I was living with Dad and Allene that I truly came to know, love, and respect my father. We traveled to Acapulco often, visited with his many friends there, and did a lot of fishing together. We also went on sailing trips to Catalina Island with Dad's friends, especially Humphrey Bogart and Errol Flynn. For me, those were wild and happy days.

Allene said,

Yes, we had some good years together, but I always felt bad
that your father never got a chance to know his children when
you were all at the critical formative ages—thanks to your
mother. She could be vindictive. When you had that appendi-
citis attack, for example, your mother did not call us; she sent
us a telegram—just enough to be in accordance with legal pro-
cedure. By the time we arrived, the operation had already been
performed, and you were recuperating in a hospital room.

Years later, when you were taken away from your mother
and made a ward of the court—I think you were around
sixteen—and you elected to come live with us, I was thrilled.
That's when we took you to Acapulco, and it was a joy for me
to see you and your dad swimming and snorkeling and really
getting to know each other for the first time. Your sisters,
Heidi and Wendy, also began to visit with us. Heidi was an
angel. Wendy was a carbon copy of her mother. Enough said
on that subject.

If it wasn't for the opportunity that I'd been given to live with
my father and Allene, I might have wound up a delinquent. Dad
was a delight to be around, but he had other things to do besides
babysit a teenager, and at times I grew bored and restless. And mis-
chievous. Witness my antics with Jimmy Mitchum.

I joined the navy in 1958, at the age of eighteen, with my friend
Jim Thornsberry. We were stationed in San Diego. Jim couldn't
swim, so they made him a lifeguard—I had to teach him to swim. I
have two thumbs when it comes to mechanics, so they made me an
engine man. I might have spent my entire hitch as an engine man if
it wasn't for my father. Dad came down to San Diego with Forrest
Tucker for a visit, and I wound up caddying for them and Admiral
Vincent A. Jaegar (I will never forget his name). The golf bag weighed
over a hundred pounds, and I discovered why when I peeked inside;
it was filled mostly with bottles of vodka.

Admiral Jaegar was appreciative, however, and he told my dad that he would take care of his boy. I deserved something better than being an engine man. I thought that this meant that I might wind up driving him in his limo and have a chance to play around with any excess lady passengers. Instead, I was transferred to the Underwater Demolition Team, UDT-11 out of San Diego, where I played around with explosives. I decided against a navy career.

After my discharge, I moved back in with my father and Allene for a while—Beryl and Getch sure didn't want me, and my sisters had been catching hell from those two while I was away. But Dad was going through a low period; he was drinking heavily, and he didn't have much money. I started accompanying him to a downtown theater to watch movies, and I began to feel a little low myself.

According to Allene, the real problem was that Dad didn't have a steady job:

He loved to work. He needed to work. When that work stopped at the termination of the *Jungle Jim* series in 1956 and Johnny had no steady employment, he just fell apart. He had too much time on his hands. He played golf, of course, at Lakeside, but the money became so tight that he could not even afford to do that often.

He began to drive to Hollywood in the afternoons and sit through double-feature films. I remember how you used to go with him, just to keep him company. Admission was free to Screen Actors Guild members. I began to play more golf tournaments, so I wasn't always—as before—there to hold his hand and keep him company. Then he began to drink more heavily. That had never really been a problem with your dad before, but it became one. I swear that when Johnny was not drinking he was the kindest, gentlest, most loving and thoughtful companion on this planet. When he started drinking heavily, it was a replay of Doctor Jekyll and Mister Hyde.

I tried everything. I spent more time with him on the golf course. That didn't work out because of his intensely competitive spirit. He wanted me to be the best, but he sure as hell didn't want me to beat him! I had to walk a very careful line.

All of this started long before your return from the navy, but it did not improve appreciably even when your father had his son back with him. He loved you and your sisters, but he could be awkward around you because he had spent so little time around children, including his own. I remember your sister Heidi ran away from home when she was about fourteen. Your mother was beside herself and had the police out searching for her. She called your father and me, but we told her that we knew nothing. After three worry-filled days, Heidi showed up at our door. She was filthy. She told us that she had been living with a Mexican family in South Los Angeles and eating nothing but frijoles and tortillas. She said that she was hungry and that she wanted to live with us. We took her in immediately, of course, and after she had showered and cleaned up, I loaned her some of my clothes. She was only fourteen, but she was already my same size.

She told us that she had run away because your mother had threatened to put her, and your sister Wendy, in a convent. Their new stepfather did not like them, and they did not like him. Their situation at home had become intolerable. I told Johnny to take Heidi to a movie; I would handle Beryl. I lied. I was so bitter about your mother by this time that I delayed calling her for a couple of days. I said to myself, "Let her sweat it out."

For sure, my sister Heidi had a rough time growing up, but she later married a fine young man who was in the U.S. Navy. She at least experienced a few years of happiness before she was killed in a car accident. Suffice it to say that of all the Weissmuller children, she was undoubtedly the purest of heart. I think of her often. I will always miss her.

During those years after my navy hitch, I faced growing-up problems. Dad was coping with depression and financial problems. I began to think about marriage, but I didn't want to rush into it. Like my father, I had never had much luck with women. But I was lonely, and in my early twenties I decided to take the plunge. My first wife was named Judy. I met her in the late 1950s, and I married her in the early 1960s. Her father was very rich, very arrogant, and very Catholic. If I wanted to marry his daughter, I would have to convert to Catholicism. What the hell? I'd never been very religious anyway. So Father Richard Madden gave me my Catholic mustard seed and taught me what I needed to know.

That marriage didn't last long. I took Judy to a convention of some sort in Ohio, and Father Madden happened to be there also. We had hotel suites with interconnecting doors. I came back early one night from a convention meeting and walked in the wrong door. There was Father Madden, on a downstroke, in bed with my wife. I returned on the next flight to Oakland, called Judy's father, and told him, "I never wanted to be a Catholic anyway. I give her back to you!"

CHAPTER 6

Tidal Wave

"The Rich Old Days Were Gone"

Word got around about my father's financial difficulties, and his friends came to his aid in such numbers that he found it hard to decide which job offers to accept. Now, you must understand that when you talk about being "penniless" in Hollywood circles, it does not mean that you have no capital assets. It just means that sometimes you can't pay the gardener. And "deprivation" is also a relative term. Dad still had property interests on Santa Catalina Island, Grandmother Elizabeth's house in Palms, his own house in Cheviot Hills, and an ongoing twenty-five-percent cut of the residuals from foreign and domestic sales of the *Jungle Jim* films. He discovered later that Roos had mortgaged some of his properties to the hilt, but he still had an interest in most.

So, he wasn't down and out, but he was bent out of shape financially. He could no longer live in the style to which he had been accustomed ever since Tarzan had first swung down from the trees onto the silver screen. We talked about this one day, and he said, "I should have listened to your mother and Allene. Both were sure that Roos was milking me dry. Yeah, it was my fault, but that did not change the fact that I was now busted. Allene and I could no longer afford to live in the style in which we had been living. We had to moderate. We had to give up some exclusive club affiliations; we had to go to work and recoup our fortune. Face it—the rich old days were gone!"

The Tragic Years

The decision to end the marriage was not an easy one. Dad and Allene loved each other. It was just that problems had been building for a long time, and the dikes finally gave way. There was no immediate divorce because neither of them wanted it, but the pressures mounted daily, and there were numerous trial separations. Allene told me that they had decided on a trial separation while I was living with them.

> You had just returned home from your hitch in the navy. So now I had two children to mother. You both needed my constant care and attention. I had always told myself that I would never leave your father, but then things just got too bad. I moved in with my mother, but I returned to the house every day while you "boys" were gone; I cleaned the place, then fixed your dinner and left it on the table for you. For six months I did that.
>
> It wasn't easy. I felt so sorry for your father. I didn't want to leave him, but I knew I had to. He begged me to stay. We separated so many times, but each time I came back Johnny would be fine for a few weeks, then fall right back into his former routine. I finally realized that there was no future for me living with the famous Johnny Weissmuller. He was just too much to handle! After our last separation, your dad moved in with María [his fifth and final wife], and I returned to the house, where I lived alone.
>
> How did all this happen? I really can't explain it, but I do know that your father was a true Gemini. When he drank, he changed personalities instantly. He once confessed to me that he drank as a crutch to instill self-confidence. Johnny had a

monumental inferiority complex. He said, "As long as I can remember, I've been ashamed of my hands and feet. They're just too big and awkward. I never know what to do with them."

It was hard for Johnny to get on a stage. Once there, he handled it fine. He loved performing for people, especially kids, but the act of getting up in front of a crowd and approaching that stage was hell for him.

You were with us for some years; then you did your hitch in the navy and came back to us again. I remember you asked me, as if apologizing for your mother, "I think I'm just too much for Mom to handle, I don't think she wants me there. Can I stay with you?" I told you that your father and I simply did not have the kind of money that your mother had, but that you were welcome to share what we had as long as you wanted to stay.

I actually stayed with your father longer than I had planned to because of you. When you married, well . . . that excuse no longer had substance.

As I said, Johnny Weissmuller could hold his liquor, but when he did tie one on, he did a number. On one of those occasions, he was arrested for drunk driving, and Peggy Linder and I took you sailing to Catalina for a few days on Peggy's boat. We did that because we didn't want you to see the newspapers for fear that it might embarrass you. We also spent a lot of time in Acapulco, just to get your father away from his drunken Hollywood friends. We would be there only a few days, and your father would beg us to take him home to see the guys: Forrest Tucker, Art LaShelle, John Wayne, Ward Bond, and the rest. Great companions, the "guys." I understand they all stopped taking showers for a while after Ward Bond succumbed while taking a cold shower.

It was your Uncle Pete, though, who was the real burden for me, and a terrible influence on your father. Pete never really left the street gangs of Chicago. He always had a racket of some kind going, mostly numbers, and he always carried a gun.

Johnny called him "the gangster," but he did try to help Pete give up the gang life by landing him a job with MGM as his stand-in. Pete also worked as a stand-in for John Wayne, but he was never a stable person. I suppose he really never got over the effects of that earlier bout with syphilis. Also, he drank like a fish. When your father didn't come home at night—which became more and more frequent—I always knew where to look for him. He was in a bar, drinking with Pete. I knew which bar to call. They always used the same one. I would call and ask the Philippino bartender, Eddie, if Mr. Weissmuller was there.

"No. He is not here."

An hour or so later, I would call and ask Eddie one more time, "Is Johnny there? Don't lie to me, Eddie!"

Long pause. "He says no."

That's when I began to give up on the marriage. It wasn't because he cheated on me or anything like that. To my knowledge, Johnny Weissmuller never cheated on me. He most certainly was not a womanizer; he was simply a big, overgrown boy who liked to laugh and tease and horse around with the boys. He had no real sense of responsibility, no understanding that marriage was not just another one of his games.

Johnny Weissmuller was neither an ideal husband nor an ideal father, but he was an experience not to be forgotten. I can say with conviction that for the first ten years of my marriage to him I was extremely happy. He brought so much into my life. I was so full of love for him. I traveled with him and met some of the most fascinating people in the world. I was absolutely fulfilled.

I often said to myself in those days, "If I die today, I will have lived a full life." I did—eventually—find love and security with another person, but what I had with your father was very special. He was truly a remarkable man. He was my Tarzan.

Black Widow

My father has been quoted as saying that the final hammer blow to his marriage to Allene was when he sold their memberships to the exclusive Lakeside Golf Club. Word got out to the newspapers, and Allene heard about it in the ladies' room at Lakeside. She tried to laugh it off, but it was obvious to some of the ladies present that she was quite upset with her husband. One of those ladies was Gertrudis María Theresia Brock Mandell née Bauman. There were other names. I have never been able to figure it all out, because she changed stories and names at the drop of a hat.

On many occasions, María herself has told this story about how she met my father:

> I knew who this woman [Allene] was, and I knew who her husband was. I was intrigued with the situation. I decided to see if I could learn more. I left the ladies' room, marched into the bar area, found Mr. Johnny Weissmuller, and introduced myself. The moment I looked into his eyes and touched his hand, I knew that this was a good man. I also knew that he was a terribly unhappy man and was married to the wrong woman. I was the right woman for him. I could make him happy. As silly and foolish as it may sound, I determined then and there that whatever machinations it might entail, and however long it might take, I was going to marry Johnny Weissmuller.

Allene recalls the incident somewhat differently:

> I don't know where that silly story came from. It makes me sound like a vamp, or a nagging, disloyal wife. I have no idea whether María was in the ladies' room or not when I was advised by some of my snickering golf partners that I probably shouldn't be in the clubhouse since I was no longer a member. I immediately phoned your father and found out it was true. He had sold our memberships, without advising me of that intention, for six thousand dollars, which he needed to

pay pressing debts to the IRS. Moreover, he had not even used the money for that purpose; he had frittered it away on some foolish scheme or another. Yeah, I was furious, and I may have even muttered a "Damn him!" or two, especially after I discovered that all of my belongings had already been removed from my locker. I was upset, but I think that is understandable. I do know that the way María tells the story simply is not true.

The Web

María was German by birth and, according to one of her stories, a titled descendant of the House of Wittelsbach. She claims that she married in her teens and lost her first husband during World War II; he died on the Russian front. From that marriage came a baby girl, named Lisa. María also said that her second husband, a flier, was shot down and killed eight months after their marriage. A lawyer friend of her first husband, who often visited María and Lisa during the war, was arrested, along with his entire family, and all were hanged, accused of being members of the resistance. María claimed that she too was arrested by the Gestapo but later released due to lack of evidence.

When World War II ended, María emigrated to the United States, where she stayed with an uncle in Santa Barbara, California. Soon afterwards, she became a U.S. citizen. She married once more, but that marriage ended in divorce. She did, however, manage to put Lisa through school, and she was proud that her daughter had received a good education. Lisa married a judge, moved to Indianapolis, and, at the time María came into Dad's life, was expecting a child. María couldn't have been happier at the prospect of becoming a grandmother. In the meantime, she was free to pursue Tarzan—which she did like the huntress that she was.

Dad really never had a chance against this tough lady. But María didn't reel him in all that easily. Although Dad was separated from Allene, he was still legally married, and even after that ended in 1963, María had a battle on her hands. When it came to marriage, Dad was gun-shy. He called one day and asked me to come over to his house and talk about it. This is not something that I like to

María and Johnny Weissmuller, artist unknown.

discuss, but I think that even then Dad realized he was failing mentally. When I asked him why in the world he wanted to get married
again, he said, "John, I feel lonely, and I need someone to take care
of me."

I replied, "Okay, Dad, but why her? Of all people, why her? Do
you really believe that nonsense about her being a German countess? This is a joke on the Strip, where she hangs out in bars. She
talks with this phony accent, and you think she is a countess? Hell,
Dad, you have better hereditary credentials than this woman does."
María, who was in the house at the time, overheard this conversation and came storming into the room, giving me hell for talking
against her. We went at it tooth and nail for a while, and she ended
the conversation with "Talk all you want, John boy, but I'm going
to get what's due me!"

Whatever the hell that meant. I don't know what she thought was "due" her, but she did eventually get Dad to the altar.

The Bite

I really doubt that my father would have married María if it had not been for the loss of his baby daughter. It happened on November 19, 1962. Heidi was driving her husband, Michael Houso, and a friend back to the naval base in San Diego, where the two men were stationed, and the car hit a soft shoulder. Michael and his friend survived. Heidi died, along with her unborn baby. She was nineteen years old. Dad was so broken up about this that even I could not get through to him. The fact that he had also lost an unborn grandchild in the accident doubled his pain. He was simply crushed. And, unfortunately, María was right there to provide him with solace and comfort. She hadn't even known Heidi, but she sensed the depth of feeling that Johnny Weissmuller had for his daughter, and she played that card for all it was worth. Dad was alone and grief-stricken, and María was there to assure him that she cared. Professional black widows probably dream about spinning their webs around this kind of gratuitous offering.

The grief that both Dad and I felt almost overwhelmed us. I don't think that either of us ever really got over the shock of Heidi's death. To the day he died, Dad cried every time her name was mentioned, and I don't think the burden on my heart will ever diminish. She was an angel when she was here with us, and I am sure that she is an angel wherever she is now.

But Dad did come around to accepting Heidi's death, slowly, and he and I became much closer for having shared that sad experience. As we became closer, I reached the age when I needed to find work, and my father helped me. He never gave me money, but he did help me to find my way in the film industry. I was given a number of small film parts; later I branched into theater work, which I much preferred.

After Dad came to terms with the trauma of losing his "baby," he began to accept some of the job offers that he was receiving. He started off by doing radio and TV work, plugging such products as

Kevo-etts, a vitamin supplement. It paid the bills, and it gave him exposure. A Hollywood agent saw him on television and called to ask that he consider a role similar to Bogart's in *The African Queen*; there was a possibility that John Huston would direct. Dad agreed to consider it, and the agent promised to send him the script. It never arrived.

My father then got into the swimming-pool business with Kurt Stier, a Chicago man reputed to be a world expert on prefabricated pools. For the use of his name, Dad was offered a substantial percentage of the company—to be called Johnny Weissmuller Steel Porcelain Pools by Alpoa. The venture started off very well, and sales were brisk, but then clients began calling and complaining that their orders had not been honored or that their pools were falling apart. Some threatened lawsuits. Dad made himself an ex-partner as quickly as he could sign his name to a release contract. Allene recollected the fiasco:

> While we were still married, your father did get into a swimming-pool venture with a crooked company. I remember that well. They accepted deposits from people, dug a hole in their backyards, then never showed up again. Johnny had gone into this without the knowledge of Roos, and we wound up in court. Fortunately, however, Johnny and I never received a penny from this bogus venture. They were simply using the Weissmuller name. We were absolved of all blame by the court on that one. Some of the other ventures Johnny got us into were not so easy. Your father was a lovable man, but he sure as hell was no businessman!

Dad kept trying. His former stuntman and good friend Paul Stader had been working on a script for some time about a wilderness-trader adventure on the Amazon. He nearly convinced "Tarzan" to take the lead role, but María vehemently objected, and the idea went the way of most ideas in Hollywood.

When Robert Wian, owner of Big Boy Franchises, heard of my father's financial difficulties from mutual friends such as Forrest

Tucker, Al Dean, and Jim Raymond, he called Dad and told him that he had found just the thing for him in Las Vegas. Caesar's Palace would be delighted to hire Johnny Weissmuller in a public-relations capacity. Wian told Dad that his name was a natural draw and that any number of big Las Vegas clubs were eager to sign him. He added that the pay and benefits were more than liberal. Dad accepted on the spot and hung up the phone. Then he placed a call to Major Riddle, president of the Dunes Hotel in Las Vegas, and booked the bridal suite. Johnny Weissmuller and Gertrudis María Theresia Brock Mandell née Bauman were married in 1963. She was forty-two, and he was fifty-nine. Forrest Tucker served as best man.

María commented later, in a televised interview, "The wedding was a grand party, and it went on, with ups and downs, for some twenty-one years. I never regretted a minute of it."

I was upset when Dad married María, but not nearly as upset as Allene. Her recollections of María are even less favorable than mine.

> She was in all the bars up and down Sunset Strip nightly. They called her the Countess, but as a joke. I am sure that is just something that she made up. But your father appeared to be getting better while living with her, so I decided to try and make my own life, alone.
>
> Your father visited with me often, however, and on one of those visits he said, "Allene, I need the medal back." Years earlier, he had given me his Olympic gold medal, set in a beautiful, slave-type, solid-gold bracelet. When I asked him why he wanted it returned, he said, "María wants it. She told me that if I didn't get it for her that she would kill me." He laughed nervously. "I think she means it!"
>
> I said, "Well, for heaven's sake—of course, John. Take the medal!" But I was so dumb that I gave him my gold bracelet also. I should at least have kept that!
>
> When I speak of "the gold medal" in the singular, I mean

just that. Most stories published state that all of Johnny Weissmuller's Olympic gold medals are in the Swimming Hall of Fame. That is not true. They are scattered to the four winds. The last one that your dad still had in his possession was the one that María wound up with. As far as I know, she still has it.

María was a demanding woman. When she was sure that I was out of town, for example, she would persuade your father to take her and a bevy of her friends to my house, where they would party all night. When I returned home, it was always to a complete shambles. So I said to him, "Johnny, you are not doing this ever again! I am not a maid, and I am not going to clean up after María. She's a complete mess! She can have her parties in her own home!"

So that was the end of that. I only met María once, and that was at your first wedding—I think in Walnut Creek. I don't recall ever having seen Maria, or spoken with her, since. Who would want to?

I knew that your father and María had met in a bar—I think the Scandia—but that is to be expected. She was a barfly. She had this accent—I don't know if it was phony or not—but I do remember that people used to laugh at her. I was embarrassed for your father. I said to him one day, "Johnny, why her? Why are you doing this?" He said, "Because I am so alone. I'm lonesome. . . ." It was tragic.

I thought to myself, "Johnny Weissmuller could have any woman in the world that he wants. He could probably marry into dignity and wealth. His name, his fame, his good looks— why this?" Who knows? I only know that María got him and trapped him in her web until the day that he died. Then she enshrined him. Some people look on this as a beautiful love story. I think it is sick.

If María had the money today, I am sure that she would install, somewhere along Acapulco's *La Costera*, a giant statue of Tarzan, replete with halo. Johnny Weissmuller was one hell of a good guy, María, but he was no saint. Neither are you.

It's true that my father was no saint, but he did deserve better than María. Why he chose to marry her is anyone's guess, but it was his decision to make.

～

It was during the María years that I decided to get married again myself. My next wife was Peggy; I don't recall her maiden name, but she sure as hell wasn't a Catholic. We lived together for a few years, and I have a daughter by her, named Heidi, after my sister. It was during this period that I started a company, with a guy named Jerry Thompson, called Sausalito Underwater Search. We didn't make a lot of money, so when I saw a newspaper advertisement for longshoremen, I applied.

Also during this period, I worked on the side as a diver for the Havaside Barge Company, which ran barges and tugboats and the like out of San Francisco. I was a "pile butt," which is what they called an operating engineer. One of the jobs I did was in San Luis Obispo, at a place called Avila. They were running big tankers in and out of there, and I had to dive down to uncouple and recouple the shackles that attached the tankers to embedded anchors. Really rough work. When I finished that job, Havaside gave me a good recommendation. Perhaps the name Johnny Weissmuller Jr. also helped—in any case, I got the job I'd seen advertised in the paper and joined the longshoremen's union, the ILWU. The competition was tough for good jobs in those days. The ad had been for seven hundred longshoremen, but seven thousand showed up. This was in 1967, and I'm still a longshoreman.

My sister Wendy is somewhat embarrassed that her brother—son of the famous Tarzan—is a longshoreman. Perhaps she saw Marlon Brando in On the Waterfront too many times. But I look on it as good, honest work. It pays well and provides excellent benefits. I can honestly say that I have made my own way. I never asked for one damned thing from my father other than his love and encouragement. And, as I said before, he never gave me money. Hell, he never even bought me a car, as most fathers who can afford it do for their teenaged sons. But he did give me his unconditional love. I have a lot of rich-kid friends who would almost have died for that. And my father also taught me the value of a sound work ethic. It sometimes occurs to me that Dad and I were the only two people in the entire Weissmuller clan who held steady jobs in the past one hundred years! That's a sobering thought.

CHAPTER 7

Ebb Tide

Lean Times

Dad's work in Las Vegas was an on-and-off sort of thing. In the meantime, he tried his hand at many other business ventures, most of them flops. This period of his life is a bit vague to me, for we never really discussed it, and María doesn't want to talk about it. When Bill Reed tried to interview her for this book, she said, "Why do you want to know all this? . . . I just don't have the time. . . . I have to go to the dentist . . . maybe a few weeks from now . . . we'll see. . . ."

We decided to give up on María. It is probably just as well, since she likely had nothing new to offer, and I'm not sure how much of what she might have said we could have believed. Her stories have changed so much over the years that it is practically impossible to determine what is fact and what is fiction. The same holds true of the countless Weissmuller minibiographies, magazine articles, and newspaper articles out there; of course, most of that material also came from María. During the last few years of Dad's life, she discovered that she could make money by selling interviews and photo sessions to any and all takers, and apparently the more bizarre the story the better the pay. One of my major reasons for writing this book is to try to put some of these "María fables" to rest.

So, because I lack firsthand information about this period in my father's life—the 1960s and '70s, when María had him securely under her thumb—I am compelled to rely on recent conversations with people who knew or worked with my father at the time and on other sources that I believe to be correct.

During these lean times, Dad would take on almost anything that would put bread on the table—such as doing a television series on swimming, making personal appearances, lending his name to a variety of commercial products—but he also found time to make voluntary contributions.

For example, in 1965, he agreed to support and promote the International Swimming Hall of Fame in Fort Lauderdale, Florida, to help out his friend Buck Dawson. His only pay was having his accommodations covered, when and if needed. The organization gave him an office with a star and his name on the door, but he seldom used it, and it became more of a storeroom than anything else. What most people who have not visited the Swimming Hall of Fame do not know is that just beyond the entrance, in the promenade, is a bronze statue of Johnny Weissmuller (almost double life-size), and imprinted in the cement walkway leading up to the statue are his footprints. When the Swimming Hall of Fame opened officially, in 1968, my father became the founding chairman of the board.

Although he was hard up for money, Dad refused a lucrative offer from a tobacco company to sponsor its product. He was dead set against smoking, because he was convinced that it was a health hazard, especially for young people. This was long before the public revelations about cancer risks and the popular crusade against smoking.

Dad tried other things instead, including, early in 1969, a franchising venture that he called Jungle Hut. His plan was to branch out into four areas: Jungle Hut Restaurants, Johnny Weissmuller's

*Buster Crabbe, Murray Rose, and Johnny Sr. give Milton Berle
a lesson in the breaststroke at the Swimming Hall of Fame.*

Safari Hut Gift Shops, Johnny Weissmuller's American Natural Food
Stores, and Johnny Weissmuller's Umgawa Club Lounges. None of
these ever really got off the ground.

In 1970, my father attended the British Commonwealth Games,
in Jamaica, where he was presented to Queen Elizabeth. She told
him how much she had enjoyed his films when she was a youngster.
In 1971, he received the American Patriot Award; and in 1972, at
the Munich Olympics, along with three other former Olympians,
he was presented with a set of sterling silver commemorative medals designed by noted sculptor Seymour Chaste for the Franklin
Mint. The medals were sold worldwide by Coca-Cola U.S.A., and
the proceeds were donated to the United States Olympic Committee.

By 1973, Dad and boxer Joe Louis were working together as
greeters at Caesar's Palace in Las Vegas. There, Dad fell off a chair
that he had been standing on and fractured his hip, marking the
beginning of a series of health problems. There is strong evidence to

Caesar's Palace.

support the idea that the accident occurred because my father had suffered his first stroke. After that, his mind began to deteriorate rapidly. He would suffer many strokes over the next few years.

Yet, despite his mental and physical ailments, in 1974 he was declared "Undefeated King of Swimming" by the International Palace of Sports, and in 1976 he somehow managed to travel to Buenos Aires to help raise money for a children's hospital.

I am a bit ashamed that I did not make a greater effort to be there for him more often during those years. But I was occupied with my work, and on the occasions that I did try to spend more time with Dad, I usually encountered a María roadblock. Reasons, excuses— I should have tried harder. At this point, Johnny Weissmuller needed all the help that he could get. A succession of hucksters wanted to use his name to promote their business schemes, so he became involved in a string of ill-fated ventures. He was an innocent afloat in a sea filled with sharks. For most of his life, my father had been violated. I should have understood that and been of more help, even if I could only offer him sympathy.

While all of this was going on, I was working in San Francisco as a longshoreman and acting in movies and on the stage. I was also getting married again. I met Diane Jones in August 1973, when I was in a play at San Francisco's Little Fox Theater. I played the part of Chief Bromden in *One Flew over the Cuckoo's Nest*. The play ran for five and a half years, and I played that part for three and a half years. I worked seven shows a week, six nights a week, for eighty-five dollars a week.

I actually met Diane three days after she had left hubby number two in Boulder, Colorado, and run away to San Francisco with her three-year-old son, Chad. She came from a well-to-do family. Her father, Walter, was a successful rancher who later built feed-and-grain elevators all over the United States and Eastern Europe. Diane was bright, educated, funny, and what is puzzling to me is why I didn't marry her sooner. We hit it off immediately, but it took us a long time to extricate ourselves from other personal relationships. I was living with another woman, and Diane was involved with two lawyers, one in San Francisco and one on the East Coast. Her father said to her, "Jesus Christ! Can't you meet anyone other than these shit-heel lawyers? I've been in litigation with lawyers my entire life!" Diane replied, "What about an unemployed actor?"

Six years later, at the Washington Square Bar and Grill in San Francisco, it all came together. I was ready. Diane was ready. I took her to Acapulco to meet Dad, my mother, and Jon Konigshofer—I think it was in October 1977—and on that trip we became engaged. We were married two years later, at the insistence of Chad. Chad and I are very close, and I have always looked on him as my own son. He jokes that he picked me to be his father and picked out our new car in the same year. That was twenty-three years ago, and Diane and I have had a good marriage. Although we didn't have children of our own, we have been blessed with three lovely grandchildren. God has been good to us.

Johnny Jr. with Chuck Hallinan during a performance of
One Flew over the Cuckoo's Nest.

Here is an interesting side note that relates incidentally to my marriage. Family friend Ted Doherty was driving my mother to Carmel for a function when he remarked, "Isn't it wonderful that since John and Diane married John has lost his stutter?" Ted told me that my mother turned to stone, and he had no idea why. He later learned that Mother had been told by her psychiatrist that hair pulling and stuttering were usually associated with inadequate parental care and nurturing—most often maternal.

As I've said, my mother was one of a kind. She always wanted her children near her on holidays, but for the rest of the year she didn't give a damn where they were or what they were doing. She would fly all of us to Acapulco and then get into the gin and verbally abuse anybody within earshot. She finally married Jon Konigshofer, and they found a vacation home in Acapulco. Jon's son died in his teens, and his daughter was killed in a riding accident. Having no other children, Jon transferred his love and affection to my mother's children and grandchildren. Jon Konigshofer was one of the dearest, most gentle men I have ever known, but, perhaps for that very reason, he sometimes drove Mother crazy. One day, she became so angry with him that she shot him between the legs. The bullet missed the target, ricocheted, and nearly hit her instead. She came steaming up to San Francisco on the next jet, crying, "Jon Konigshofer tried to *kill* me!"

Mother told me many times that she wished she had never left my father, "who was a *good* man."

My father was a good man, but he'd also been a relatively poor man for some time. There is no worse sin in high society (especially Hollywood high society) than to be "poor." The following story illustrates my point. During this general period, I was doing a lot of sailing, and in 1977 I entered the Trans-Pacific Yacht Race from Long Beach to Honolulu. After the race, I took the crew to the

Outrigger Canoe Club for drinks and dinner. I introduced myself and told the maître d' that my father had been a member since 1946 and had told me that I could use the club's facilities under his name. The maître d' answered, "Of course. Please come in, Mr. Weissmuller. It is a pleasure to have you aboard."

We were seated at one of the best tables in the place. A few minutes later, however, a waiter scurried over and said, "I'm sorry, Mr. Weissmuller, but we will have to ask you to leave. It seems that your father has not paid his dues here since 1946."

The Outrigger Canoe Club charges very steep dues. (Diane and I later spent a lot of time there as guests of the Kahanamoku family, and with Diane's "Honolulu Daddy," Stafford Kelly.) It is true that almost everybody loved my dad, but in that crowd only two kinds of people did not pay dues: those who were too rich to really give a damn, and those who were broke. I think Dad started out in the former category and wound up in the latter. The word was out. The Old Man was out of a job.

Downhill Run

María said in one of her published accounts that things began to go wrong after Dad fell and broke his hip at Caesar's Palace. He was treated for that injury at Nevada Memorial Hospital, and there he had the first of a series of heart attacks and strokes. María added, "He always seemed to recover fully; he was still a strong and handsome man . . . but the worry was there, always, that the next one could be the last one. He fought it day in and day out, never admitting to himself that he wasn't still the Tarzan of old. That was the sad part to me. He simply refused to grow old gracefully."

That part is true. What is also true is that María, sensing that her meal ticket was in jeopardy, contacted her personal lawyers, who drafted for her a will that stated

I appoint my said Wife, MARIA WEISSMULLER, Executrix of my Will, to serve without bond or other security for the faithful performance of her duties. Should my said Wife predecease me or be unable or unwilling to serve as Executrix of my Will, then I appoint my daughter, LISA WEISSMULLER, as Executrix of my Will, to serve without bond or other security for the faithful performance of her duties.

The will also stipulated that Johnny Weissmuller's "daughter," Lisa Weissmuller, and his son, Johnny Weissmuller Jr., would share equally in the proceeds of his estate, but no mention was made of Wendy or anyone else.

My father would never have drafted such a will if he had been in his right mind. In the first place, he would never have left his natural daughter, Wendy, out of his will. In the second place, he would have named me, his firstborn child, the executor of his will, should María predecease me. There is no evidence that I, or my lawyers, or my record-search specialists can find that Lisa was ever legally adopted by my father. There may be such a document, but I have spent many thousands of dollars trying to locate it, and my specialists affirm that it does not exist in any public archive that they can find. Even Jim Fox, the former head of the FBI in New York, could find no evidence that Lisa was ever adopted by my father. I've asked Lisa repeatedly to provide proof of this, and she has yet to produce it. If she ever does, I am sure that it will be of Mexican origin, jotted down on a scrap of paper; some Mexican lawyers and judges can be bought for a case of Corona beer. (By this, I do not mean to imply that there are not good, decent, and honorable lawyers and judges in Mexico. But legal papers can be, and often are, bought and sold. Mexico has no monopoly on this kind of thing. It happens in the United States—indeed, in countries around the world—as well.)

If I have ever witnessed a setup, this was a setup. María and her lawyers drafted this will, shoved it in front of a man who had just suffered a stroke (and who was probably already one taco shy of a fiesta), and said, "Sign it." Dad signed it.

Allene shares this opinion:

When your father fell off that chair in Caesar's Palace, everybody said, "Oh, he was just drunk!" I don't believe that for one moment. This man could handle vast amounts of alcohol and never stagger or fall or even lose speech control. I think he fell off that chair because he had his first stroke. It was followed by many others, the worst being when María— apparently wanting to have some freedom—sent him alone to visit a friend at the Balboa Bay Club on Balboa Island, California. Johnny really had a bad one there, and he didn't even know where he was for days. It was after that that he went into the Motion Picture Home. He should have stayed there, with professional help, until he died. I will always feel bad about that. Anyway, I am convinced that it was a series of strokes—not alcohol induced—that eventually took his mind— and his body.

I myself am not convinced that it was a series of strokes that initially affected Dad's mental condition. Allene often told the story about the time, when I was living with her and Big John during my midteens, that Johnny came home after being out all night. She and her mother encountered him at the front door as they were leaving for a golf tournament. Allene had been pacing the floor all night, worried sick, and when she asked him where he had been, he said, "I got lost on the way home, and I was in an oil field and went to sleep." Even though, to her knowledge, he had never cheated on her, Allene didn't believe him, but her mom said, "I believe him. Look at the oil and tar on his car, on the tires."

I later discussed this with Allene, and she said that perhaps my father was actually losing it way back then. The more we talked about it, the more she remembered other episodes that just weren't quite right. And so did I.

My father had a big La-Z-Boy sofa in his house on Lorenzo Street in Cheviot Hills, and we used to sit there for hours watching television and telling lies. On one of those occasions, Dad told me a whopper. He insisted that he had an intuitive knack for eyeballing people—for picking up on good or bad vibrations. He attributed this ability to experiences he'd had in his youth when he and Pete were dabbling in the numbers game and laundering money for some of the New York big boys. He said that to do this sort of thing you had to be street-smart and learn how to size a guy up. He swore to me that he could tell in a microsecond whether a guy was good or bad.

A few days later, we were out on the golf course. He was scheduled to play in a foursome, and I was toting his bags. As we approached the other three guys, Dad started muttering, and I asked him what was going on. He said, in a low voice, "That guy on the right there—watch him. He's no good."

I didn't know what the hell he was talking about, but I did keep my eye on this dude, and while eavesdropping I learned that he was some kind of Hollywood producer. And he *was* an obnoxious sonofabitch: loudmouthed, belligerent, bombastic. But so were the other two guys—Hollywood types all. Six of one, half dozen of the other, as far as I could tell. But Dad had his mind made up, and he complained to me constantly about the producer. If the guy had been Mahatma Mohandas Gandhi himself, Dad would have found something about him to distrust. Finally he whispered to me, "I've had it!" Then he made some excuse about a sore arm, said that he wasn't feeling well, and excused himself from the round. As we walked away, he said, "See, John? I really had that guy pegged, didn't I?"

I may have been a callow youth, but even I could see that Dad had staged the whole thing. It was so damned transparent. He just wanted to impress me with what a perceptive, "street-smart" guy he was. I thought to myself, "Christ, Dad! Every crook and con artist in town knows you're the easiest mark around. You probably couldn't pick up on John Dillinger if you spotted him in front of a bank with a gun in his hand. I may be only seventeen, but I'm already more street-smart than you've ever been or ever will be."

I was embarrassed for my father. He didn't have to make up stories like that to impress me or to gain my admiration. But now I see it for what it was. Dad was losing it. He was no longer the strong, confident, perceptive man that he once was, but he wanted to be. He wanted to see himself as the Tarzan of old—"Tarzan always smell bad man!" He wanted me to acknowledge that he still had it. It wouldn't have surprised me much if Dad had let out with a Tarzan yell, right there on the golf course. It would have embarrassed me, but it wouldn't have surprised me.

That was strange behavior. And I have been told by others who knew my father well in the late 1950s and early '60s that they too occasionally noticed strange behavior on his part. The more I think about it, the more I suspect that the series of strokes that Dad later experienced simply accelerated a preexisting condition.

My father's last public appearance was in 1976, when he gave his famous Tarzan yell for a group of New Yorkers while being inducted into the Body Building Guild Hall of Fame. It was a grueling day for him. María said that he was so exhausted after the event that he turned to her and said, "Honey, I'm getting so old, I think we should go home right away."

Shortly after their arrival back in Las Vegas, Dad had another stroke, and María asked Lisa to assist her in moving my father to Los Angeles. She also called me. Fortunately, at the time, I was a council member of the San Francisco Screen Actors Guild, and I was also on the Executive Council, Minorities Committee, for the National Board of Directors for that organization. Pulling a few strings, I managed to get Dad into the Motion Picture and Television Country Home and Hospital in Woodland Hills, California. The Motion Picture Home was a facility for members of the Screen Actors Guild who needed nursing care. It was there that my father's mind began to fade dramatically.

Days of listless behavior were followed (according to María) by bursts of energy—for example, he'd do the Tarzan yodel. Bizarre, and no doubt groundless, paparazzi articles described him swinging on chandeliers and jumping in and out of the beds of elderly female residents. When Mike Oliver heard that story, he was furious.

*The country house at the Motion Picture
and Television Fund Home.*

I knew your father extremely well, and I considered him one of my best friends. We would sometimes drink and party together for days on end, telling jokes and laughing like kids and completely ignoring guests who became aggressive and belligerent. During all that time, I never knew him to behave in any manner other than as a perfect gentleman.

In fact, the only time I ever heard Johnny Weissmuller raise his voice was when the mayor of Acapulco, at my instigation, offered him the keys to the city. María, who was with him at the time, screamed, "What are you trying to do? Blackmail us?"

I said, "No, María, we are not trying to blackmail you. We are simply offering you the keys to the city." María opened her mouth once more, and Johnny jumped up from his seat and shouted, "Shut up!" María shut up. Tarzan had spoken.

Bed hopping? Swinging from chandeliers? Utter foolishness. I am sure that that is something María made up, because she wanted him to herself in Acapulco.

When I reminded Allene about this episode, she said,

I was quite upset when I learned that Johnny was having a series of strokes and had gone into the Motion Picture Home. The next I heard, he was down in Acapulco, with María.

I don't believe that story about him being evicted. That was María's fabrication. She just didn't want him there. She wanted him alone, with her, in Acapulco. He was hers, and she would share him with nobody.

Twelve years after I remarried, I called your father while he was still in the Motion Picture Home. I said, "Johnny, do you know who this is?" He said, "Of course I know who this is. You're Allene, my wife. Why aren't you here with me?"

That shows perception, but it also says something about how his mind was wandering. I understand, from other mutual friends, that Johnny often called María "Allene." That must have driven her up a vine. No wonder she hated me.

I have read so many accounts—stated as gospel—that Johnny Weissmuller's addiction to drink was the cause of the strokes that eventually took his life. I knew this man as well as anybody in the world knew him—perhaps better. He was not an alcoholic; he was an occasional heavy drinker. As I mentioned earlier, he would go on drinking binges, which sometimes made him belligerent and hard to handle, but this was not a constant thing.

When he had a film to make, he would say, "Okay, that's it. I'm going into training," and then he wouldn't touch a drop of alcohol, even beer or wine, for sometimes months at a time. His self-control amazed me. He could turn off drinking like turning off a faucet. Moreover, he would lose weight and get into good shape very rapidly. That's not the mark of an alcoholic. And he was also a big eater, which most alcoholics are not. He always loved animals, but when our poodle snatched his morning steak off his plate one day, I thought he would kill the dog.

I am convinced that what Allene said is true. I doubt that my father made any remarkable outbursts in the Motion Picture Home, but María insisted that he did and said that she and Lisa were concerned about possible damage, which they might have to pay for if Dad were to continue his "escapades." She wanted to take him to Acapulco. Mother and Jon Konigshofer maintained homes in Carmel, California, and Acapulco, and, with the help of Mike and Rita Oliver, they found Dad and María a modest rental house. Swallowing her pride, María accepted.

They stayed in the rental house for a few years, but nurses were impossible to keep. Mike Oliver tried to help, but he said that María threw all the nurses out, using abusive language. He sent in a corps of nurses from the army, the navy, and the civilian hospitals. To no avail. María chased them all away.

By 1980, Dad was getting weaker and less active each day, and they moved him to the Los Flamingos Hotel. According to the hotel's Adolfo Santiago,

I talked with María, Mike and Rita Oliver, and others, and we agreed that your father should come here and stay in this hotel that he loved so much. We put him in the Round House, above, near the pool. By that time, he was weak and ailing, but he could still get around. I remember how much he liked Mexican food, even the *picante*—the really hot stuff. His drink at that time was a Bull Shot. A tough drink, but he held his liquor well. He never got aggressive, only happy. Everybody loved your father. I took care of him for four years, but some time in 1984, when he became too sick, María moved him back into their home, and he was put on a respirator.

María said that after that "only part of my Johnny was there. A part of his mind had left and gone somewhere else. But, every once in a while, he'd look me in the eye, and I'd see that vital life that used to be there. He'd smile as if he knew what I was thinking and say, 'It's okay, honey. Even Tarzan has to grow old.'"

How much of that is María's fabrication we may never know, but going by my personal recollections and those of others who knew my father, his final days were not pleasant.

While Dad was still in the hospital, Mother sent us tickets to fly down to Mexico and stay with her. When we got to the hospital, we found two old Mexican women sleeping on the floor by Dad's bed. We were told that María seldom, if ever, came to the hospital. She and Lisa were at the discotheques every night. The care that Dad was receiving was absolutely shameful. The facilities were dirty, there was blood everywhere, and Dad just lay there, usually totally naked and exposed; doctors and nurses rarely came around to administer professional care.

We confronted María and told her that we wanted to take Dad back to the United States and place him in a decent hospital. Perry Dudden, a friend of Diane's, offered to fly his big Beechcraft down to Acapulco and bring Dad back. Dad wanted to come with us. By this point, he'd been wanting to leave Acapulco, and María, for some time. In the late 1970s, before he lost his ability to speak, he begged me to take him "home." He whispered, "They're bad, Johnny. They're bad people. Please take me home. I want to go back and see the guys. I want to be with the guys." He did not realize that he had outlived most of the "guys"—including Forrest Tucker, John Wayne, Ward Bond, Errol Flynn, Humphrey Bogart, and the other members of that memorable crew.

Wendy commented that even after Dad became unable to speak, his eyes would light up, the cardiac machine would go wild, and tears would stream down his face the moment that I stepped into the room. He loved me very much. In his eyes, I could do no wrong. I also loved him very much. But here I was, faced with something that I simply could not combat successfully.

I tried my best. I talked it over with Diane, and she agreed that we would take him into our home and get private nurses for him rather than place him in a hospital. We could put him on my longshoreman's insurance; as long as a member of my family was living under my roof, that person would be covered by my insurance policy. I discussed all of this with María—in fact I pleaded with her—but she absolutely refused to cooperate. She insisted on keeping Dad in Acapulco.

We met with lawyers, and they told us that there was nothing we could do. María was Johnny Weissmuller's lawful wife, and she had the legal right to dictate the terms of residence and care of her husband.

One of those lawyers was Arlo Mayne, legal counsel for the Ashland Oil Company, which at that time was one of the world's largest independent oil companies. Both he and Orin Atkins, the company's founder and CEO, admired my father very much. Orin even went so far as to speculate about sending down a few of his dark-suited bodyguards in his corporate jet to kidnap Dad from Maria's home. I think he would really have done it if I had agreed. By that time, I was getting so desperate that I almost did.

After investigating every reasonable recourse available to us, we gave up the fight with sad hearts. We had just read this line of María's (I think it was in the *National Enquirer*): "...and my husband's last request...when we finally realized that he was dying...was to be buried in Acapulco." Sure, María.

Just before we returned to San Francisco, Diane asked María if there was anything more that we could do. She gave us a broken breathing apparatus and asked if we could buy Johnny a new one. We tried to do so after we returned home, but we were told that we had to have a doctor's prescription to purchase such a device. Diane phoned María and asked her to get us a prescription. María said, "Oh, just forget it. It's probably too late now to do much good anyway."

Over the course of the next few months, we made a few more trips to Acapulco to visit Dad and to reason with María. To no avail. Our friend Ted Doherty and his sidekick, Susie Allen, accompanied us on many of these trips. My father dearly loved Susie; she always sat next to him, and he'd steal her glass of scotch if she wasn't guarding it carefully. It became a joke between them. Susie is a jock. She swims to Alcatraz, relays the English Channel, does the Iron Man. Dad loved to talk with her about swimming. They were great buddies.

Then Ted and Susie stopped accompanying us to Acapulco because, they told me, they simply hated María and Lisa, and when María called my father by her pet name for him, "Woosie," it drove them up the wall. Most of Dad's other friends also stopped visiting him. None of them could stand María and Lisa. One of my friends called them "worse than Euro-trash." But, whatever they are, I know that they never really helped my father. They helped themselves.

From there, it was all downhill. Dad and María had no money, so María began to sell the story of "Tarzan's life" to various publications (including the *National Enquirer*). These stories would be illustrated with pictures of Dad on his deathbed, emaciated, wearing a death grin. It was revolting. Still, I think but for that they would have starved.

It amazes me to this day that it was my mother who put a stop to it. She was upset by the fact that María and Lisa were selling this stuff to publications she thought were "sleazy," and she was especially peeved that Lisa was passing herself off in those stories as "Weissmuller's daughter." Furthermore, Lisa often passed herself off around Acapulco as my sister Wendy, and while using that pseudonym she infected a number of beach boys with gonorrhea. Wendy never really got over that. Private gossip soon became public gossip, and Wendy not only refused to ever visit Acapulco again but also became a veritable recluse. Although this scandal was not of her making, she was so embarrassed that she did not want to be seen in public.

Beryl was furious, and on a trip to Acapulco she confronted Lisa (in María's presence), saying, "You're not Johnny's daughter, so stop doing that. Johnny Weissmuller had only two daughters and one son in his lifetime, and I am the mother of all three. I sure as hell never carried you in my womb for nine months. Now you have a perfectly good mother sitting here, so why are you trying to borrow my Johnny as a father? If you want attention that badly, why don't you trot on down to the town square and set yourself on fire!"

Mom was a tough lady, but she said that she would rather pay than see my father deprived of anything he needed. She visited him often in Acapulco and sent money on a regular basis; she hoped, I suppose, that this would inspire María and Lisa to peddle fewer trash articles about "her Johnny." Dad and Beryl's divorce had been acrimonious, but she obviously still loved him—though Dad didn't make it easy for her.

María brought "Woosie" to my mother's home one day for a visit, and Beryl met them at the door. Dad stared at her for a long while, as if trying to remember something, and then he finally asked, "Who are you?" She replied, "Why, John, I'm Beryl, your ex-wife. I'm the mother of your children!" Dad said, "Oh no you're not!" That must have broken Beryl's heart.

My mother was a remarkable woman, but even she could do little to break the stranglehold that María and Lisa had on my father. He was "theirs." They were making money from his continued existence—no matter how painful that was to him—and they weren't about to let him go.

Recently I heard that Lisa was deported from Cuba to Mexico on some charge or another, spent some time in a Mexican jail, and then ended up in a mental institution. She was finally deported to Los Angeles, where she was arrested for vagrancy. There were also some problems in Las Vegas. Police officials there and in Acapulco contacted us, thinking that we could possibly be of some help. I believe that help at this point is out of the question. I can only hope that Lisa was booked under some name other than Weissmuller.

Lisa's misadventures in Cuba and Mexico and Los Angeles and Las Vegas are a matter of record. An attorney friend of mine told me that Lisa once tried to enlist his wife in a prostitution ring. This woman has been an embarrassment to me for as long as I can remember. She is more detrimental to our family image than her mother and possibly somewhat deranged. I will not permit these two

The twenty-one-gun salute.

individuals to represent themselves as spokespersons for my father. He deserves better than that.

⁓

Dad spent the last day of his life in a hospital bed that had been installed in the Acapulco house. He died a lonely and broken man. Tarzan had battled his last lion—and it was even bigger than Jackie. The date was January 20, 1984. Johnny Weissmuller was seventy-nine years old.

At my father's funeral in Acapulco, John Gavin (actor and American ambassador to Mexico) officially represented his country. Linda Christian and José Estrada, one of Dad's stunt doubles, were the only other personalities of note present.

In another article, published just after the funeral, María said that "Woosie's" last words to her were "My darling María. I do love you so." Good trick, since my father had tubes in his belly and tubes in his throat and had not spoken an intelligible word during the last year or so of his life.

At the memorial service for Johnny Sr. in Beverly Hills, 1984.
From left to right: Lisa Bauman, Wendy Weissmuller,
Heidi Weissmuller (Johnny Sr.'s granddaughter), Diane Weissmuller,
Johnny Weissmuller Jr., and Arthur Lake.

Not My People

Diane and I were in Seattle working on a newspaper article when
Mother called to tell us that Dad had died. She said that María had
told her that he had to be buried within twenty-four hours and that
he was being buried in a beautiful spot overlooking the ocean,
which he had loved. We had no way of getting to Acapulco in time
for the burial and the memorial, but we certainly heard about it
from many upset friends. They all described it as a circus; there was
a parade, with a dwarf leading a defecating chimpanzee and Tarzan
yells blaring repeatedly from a loudspeaker. The priest had trouble
conducting the mass because of the pandemonium.

I don't think the "circus" paid off for María—she was likely
counting on a lot of media—because she phoned shortly afterwards
and informed us that she was planning another memorial for Dad,
this time at the Church of the Good Shepherd in Beverly Hills. We
could hardly wait to see that one. Anyway, Diane, Wendy, my

CITY OF LOS ANGELES

IN TRIBUTE

*THE LOS ANGELES CITY COUNCIL EXTENDS ITS
DEEPEST SYMPATHY TO YOU IN THE PASSING OF
YOUR LOVED ONE*

JOHNNY WEISSMULLER

*IN WHOSE MEMORY ALL MEMBERS STOOD IN TRIB-
UTE AND REVERENCE AS THE COUNCIL ADJOURNED
ITS MEETING OF JANUARY 25, 1984.*

SINCERELY,

ELIAS MARTINEZ, CITY CLERK

Presented by

COUNCILWOMAN PEGGY STEVENSON

Seconded by

COUNCILMAN GILBERT W. LINDSAY

daughter, Heidi, and my mother all flew to Los Angeles for the event. Diane and I stayed with Paul and Marilyn Stader.

The memorial service started at nine o'clock in the morning, so we were amazed to see women there wearing negligees and sequined cloches; they were also rouged and bejeweled. They looked like extras sent by central casting for a *Moulin Rouge* scene, but they were María and Lisa's friends. We were terribly embarrassed. María and Lisa were making a carnival out of this and blatantly soliciting press interviews.

I ducked out of sight. As I hid in a corner, an old man came up to me and introduced himself as a member of Grandpa Weissmuller's "other" family. He was the first of that clan whom I had met, and I was intrigued. I didn't get a chance to speak with him for as long as I would have liked, however, because the press found me. When I started to head outside with the reporters for an interview, Lisa saw me and screamed, "There he is!" She raced to the door with her ladies of the evening/morning in tow. Mother and Paul Stader blocked her exit, and she was furious. María interceded, calmed Lisa down, and insisted that she had everything under control. She said she had invited members of the German press to her apartment, and she'd like us to join them. But we had a small get-together of our own planned, so we begged off.

Before everyone dispersed, there was a twenty-one-gun salute by the United States Marines, arranged by Senator Ted Kennedy. Twenty-one-gun salutes are generally reserved for presidents or other heads of state, but somehow Ted Kennedy managed to do this for Johnny Weissmuller. It was a touching and gracious gesture in what seemed a sea of embarrassment and humiliation. We will be forever grateful to Ted Kennedy for this tribute to my father. Both María and I were then presented with an American flag.

A short while later, I was in Santa Barbara for a yacht race, sitting in the bar at the yacht club, when Robert Mitchum came and sat down beside me. "Johnny, I'm so sorry about your father. I heard there were ladies in their underwear at Big John's funeral." I just shook my head and said, "Yeah, but at least it didn't wind up on the cover of the *Enquirer*. It's sure good to see you again, Mitch. I guess I should never have let María disgrace Dad that way. Those people she invited sure weren't *my* people."

⌒

When Diane and I got another chance to return to Acapulco, we traveled with a friend of Diane's from her Stephens college days. Jackie Daniell (everybody called her "Jack Daniel's") is dead now, but back then she often traveled with us. She was very close to Diane's son, Chad, and she loved my father.

Upon our arrival in Acapulco, we were subjected to another shock. María had told us—and had even stated it in a story published in numerous magazines—that her husband and my father had been buried in a lovely spot overlooking the ocean. She also claimed that she would sit there in the evenings, watching the sun go down, feeling happy that her dear "Woosie" was there with her in spirit, enjoying the same scene.

In María's description, my father's resting place sounded marvelous; so, in the company of Adolfo Santiago of the Hotel Los Flamingos, we visited the gravesite, which was in the Panteón Valle de la Luz, a cemetery located in an obscure valley. I was stunned. Diane tells me that she and Jackie had to hold me up to keep me from collapsing.

It was the most god-awful place I have ever seen. There were pigs and chickens and goats and cows running amok among piles of animal manure and human feces. The place was littered with rusty cans, broken bottles, and scraps of clothing hanging on bushes and weeds. I would not have buried a mongrel dog there. To cap it off, Dad's name was misspelled on his tiny gravestone, which was half buried in the ground. We had to brush the dirt off to read it. In a state of despair and dismay, the four of us returned to the Hotel Los Flamingos. A stiff drink—actually a few stiff drinks—was in order.

I was in tears. Jackie told Diane that she was worried about me. She had never before seen a man in such emotional pain. But along with the intense pain in my heart there was a deep and abiding anger. "Countess" María of Wittelsbach had not only trashed my

Diane and Johnny Jr.

father's name, but she had also trashed my father's body (when it was no longer of commercial use to her), tossing it into a miserable potter's field. I have never forgiven María for that desecration. Nor will I. Diane and I left what little money we could afford with Mike and Rita Oliver to pay for the cleaning and upkeep of Dad's gravesite, and, with Jackie, we returned to San Francisco.

Some time later, by sheer accident, we ran into a man named Porfirio Flores Ayala, of Cuernavaca, at Perry's in San Francisco, of all places. He told us that he was the owner of the Panteón Valle de la Luz Cemetery. We told him our story, and he promised to spruce up the site.

I went back to being a longshoreman, and I tried to forget. I will, of course, never forget. It was around this time that I determined to write a book that would, once and for all, destroy the María and Lisa myths and charades.

Reflections

There are probably a hundred more stories that I could tell you about my father, but they would all simply illustrate and confirm the same thing: he was a big, happy, laughing giant of a man. Life to him was a game. Sometimes he played the game well and sometimes not so well, but he always played to win.

Johnny Weissmuller had what modern-day cynics may label a simplistic philosophy, but generations of his fans have understood it and embraced it. To paraphrase, "A man should stand where God places him—jungle trails or Hollywood streets—and fight for those things in which he believes."

There was never any doubt in Johnny Weissmuller's mind about the outcome of the battle. The bad guys lose. The good guys win. That was the central thread of his philosophy, and he fought for it all of his life, on screen and off. Simplistic? I find it perceptive and refreshing. It is timely. It is cogent. We need to get back to the basic values of Tarzan. Our children need to hear less about villains and cowardly terrorists and more about peaceful men of courage and honest-to-God heroes. We owe them that.

Many a friend has come up to me over the years and told me what a great man my father was. One voiced the opinion that Johnny Weissmuller was one of the greatest athletes of his century, and then he commented, "They killed him, you know. It's a pity that Hollywood killed Tarzan." My first thought was that Bö Roos, María, Lisa, Uncle Gordon, and other members of his mercenary family were more responsible for Johnny Weissmuller's death than Hollywood, but I knew what he meant. My father was, in his mind, Tarzan. Allegorically speaking, Hollywood did kill my father. I thought about that for a moment. I have little doubt that Hollywood contributed to the pressures that hastened the demise of Johnny Weissmuller, and most certainly Hollywood was guilty of murdering at least one of his marriages. Certainly, the smoking gun may be found in the hands of dozens of producers, directors, and financially driven executives who pushed for ever more jungle footage at the expense of Dad's sanity and health. But kill Tarzan? Impossible!

One only has to see the excitement in the eyes of children as they watch the Ape Man swing from a vine; hear the soft gasps of female moviegoers as the ruggedly handsome King of the Jungle takes command of Jane in Disney's 1999 animated *Tarzan*; or overhear Anita, a clerk at the confectionary counter at Neiman Marcus, ask Diane if her father-in-law really was Tarzan. Those moments put that blasphemy to rest.

"Hey! Ain't nobody ever gonna kill Tarzan! Right, Dad?"

"Umgawa, Son."

Johnny Weissmuller will always be Tarzan, just as Humphrey Bogart will always be Rick. Some things are not meant to change.

Johnny Sr.'s grave marker in Acapulco, Mexico.

REQUIEM

Jardines del Tiempo, Acapulco, Mexico

Diane and I visited the grave of my father in April of 2001. The plot was beautiful—carpeted with well-manicured green grass that would do justice to a major golf course. There was a new headstone on the grave proper, as well as a large cement and bronze plaque fronting the whole. We were delighted.

As we were about to go to the cemetery's small office and inquire about the history of this change, we met an old man who was obviously a caretaker. We identified ourselves and told him that we were interested in the history of the cemetery, especially in the history of a man named Johnny Weissmuller. "Do you remember this man? Do you know something about the circumstances of his burial?" we asked.

"Of course I remember," the caretaker replied.

I was there, and I buried Johnny Weissmuller. That was in 1984, and I have been working in this cemetery since 1979. In those days, this was not a beautiful place, as you see it now. There were weeds and cactus plants instead of manicured lawns, and there were also many cows and goats and pigs.

I especially liked the pigs. Nobody knows this story except you and me, but I personally buried, over the years, a number of pigs here in open graves. They had died, for one reason or another, and had no decent place to rest. I placed them in the graves of humans and put dirt over them before I lowered the casket into the grave. I am sure the dead persons did not mind.

Perhaps they were thankful for the company. It always amused me to see people come here on The Day of the Dead and place food, lovingly, on the graves of my pigs.

We asked the man if he knew why Tarzan, a famous man, hadn't been buried in a better place. He shook his head and said,

I have no way of knowing. Perhaps his wife did not have enough money. Perhaps it was the only place available. In those days, the graveyard was called Valle de la Luz. It was open to the public and was very primitive. It was not enclosed, as you see it now, and the grounds were dirt and mud and scrub. Cows and goats and chickens and pigs roamed here at will. I used to grab cows by the tail and hustle them out of the place. People drove by and reported that a crazy man, half naked, was abusing cows by twisting their tails. The management then insisted that I wear a shirt.

This place was so open to the public in those days that drunken drivers used to bring their cars here and race around the lanes between the graves. Once, I recall, some drunken locos threw a little boy into an empty grave, and he broke his leg. Another time, a car ran over another young boy who worked for me. The officials caught the people responsible, and they were forced to pay a great deal of money to settle a lawsuit.

After that, the company that controlled the cemetery collected money from all of the people who had family buried here in *tumbas* and *criptas,* built a wall around the place, placed a guard gate, and completely regardened the plots—as you now see. At that time, they changed the name of this graveyard from Panteón Valle de la Luz to Jardines del Tiempo.

Then we said to the caretaker, "Can you tell us about Johnny Weissmuller's burial ceremony?"
Thinking for a moment, he answered,

Yes, of course, I remember it well. As I said before, I was the man in charge of burying him. What stands out, at least in my mind, is the fact that for a man of such importance there were fewer than thirty people attending. I was also personally embarrassed that such a man would be buried in a plot of dirt and mud. It was not a pretty place in those days. If only these hills could talk, they would tell you stories that you would not believe. I have seen it all. I remember it all, as if it were yesterday.

That day at the cemetery, we were intrigued to see a red rose, a bit wilted from the Acapulco sun, on Johnny Weissmuller's grave. We asked the old man if he knew who had placed the rose there. As he arranged other, artificial, flowers around the grave to enhance our photographs, he replied, "I have no way of knowing, because so many people come here to visit the *tumba* of this fine man. I think they loved him very much."

Yes, I am sure they did. For all his faults, the entire world loved Tarzan. Rest in peace, Tarzan. Rest in peace, my father.

APPENDIX

Potpourri

THE MYTHS

The following are excerpts from a book by David Fury titled *Johnny Weissmuller: Twice the Hero:*

- The whole situation [at the Motion Picture Home] was resolved when Johnny and María *jointly* [italics are mine] decided to move to Acapulco. . . .

- One publication wrote about Johnny in his forced retirement: "The once robust six-foot-three Olympic champion may be thin and weak, but his wife Maria is encouraged by his progress the past year. . . . It is evident that constant love and care have brought Weissmuller through another year."

  The article of course bespoke the love and care of Maria, who stuck with Johnny in these toughest of times. For better or worse, richer or poorer . . . they had all of these situations in the final years of their two decades as husband and wife.

- Despite his valiant battle that lasted more than six years to recover from the big stroke of 1977, the war was finally lost on Friday evening, January 20, 1984, when Johnny Weissmuller passed away at his home in Acapulco. A spokesperson from the Acapulco Sinai Hospital, where Johnny had been treated as an outpatient from time to time, listed the official cause of death as pulmonary edema, or a blockage of the lungs. Meanwhile, Dr. Eustasio Ordaz Parades, the Weissmuller family physician, offered the opinion that he died of cerebral thrombosis—blood clotting of vessels in the brain (Dr. Parades had also been the personal physician of the eccentric billionaire Howard Hughes). . . .

- Johnny's last wishes were that he be buried in Acapulco. . . .

I know David Fury, and he is a good and decent man. It is not his fault that—as evidenced in the chapter titled "A Final Love: Johnny and Maria"—he became one of the many who were caught up in the mythical web that the Black Widow has spun so successfully for so many years. It is also not his fault that in the chapter titled "A Precious Gem Called Beryl," he faithfully records every detail of a fairy-tale romance that has been "documented" in print for over fifty years. The man used what he had to work with. Unfortunately, he went to the wrong well to draw his water. There was only one "gem" among the wives of Johnny Weissmuller, and her name is Allene Weissmuller McClelland née Gates. If only she could have endured the agonies that my father put her through and been there to support him during the declining years of his life. Had she been able to do so, this story would have had a different ending. The difference would have been somewhat akin to the difference between heaven and hell.

LONGSHOREMAN AND WIFE

Unlike my sister Wendy, my wife is not at all unhappy that I am a long-shoreman. It pays well, and the benefits are substantial. Diane had to have a liver transplant in 1992 (the organ was donated by a seventeen-year-old Mexican boy), and she has just won a bout with cancer. California Pacific Medical Center, where her operation was performed, has the highest survival rate for organ-transplant patients, and her doctors say that the immune suppressants that they have given her have a three-percent incidence of cancer, which is very small indeed. Diane has undergone chemotherapy and radiation treatments, and she's now a living testimony to the fact that there is life after a transplant. One can only imagine what all of this has cost, but the Longshoremen's Union has paid at least ninety-nine percent of it. Thank God! Still and all, I just hit sixty, and I'm sure looking forward to retirement.

THERE ARE TWO OF ME

I am not the only Johnny Weissmuller Jr. around these days. There is another guy who goes by that name; his checks are imprinted "Johnny Weissmuller Jr.," and he is apparently doing quite well for himself financially by using my name. He always pays by check; he drives a Ferrari, charters airplanes, and at last report was trying to purchase a hotel in Lake Tahoe, stating that he was the legitimate, one-and-only son of Johnny Weissmuller Sr. His credentials were impeccable. Luckily, the owner of the hotel knows me, and he kicked the bastard out. Then he phoned and told me to watch my back.

There was also an account in a Kansas City newspaper about an old prostitute and card dealer who had done some time in prison. She claimed that the biggest thrill of her life was when Johnny Weissmuller Jr. tipped her fifteen hundred dollars. It sure wasn't me—I would have remembered.

In June of 2001, *Entertainment Weekly* published the "log" of Bonny Lee Bakley, which lists Johnny Weissmuller Jr. as one of her clients—or at least one of her targeted marks. She described Johnny Weissmuller Jr. as a rich playboy who had a home in an exclusive neighborhood, a swimming pool, and so forth.

I do not reside within that exclusive zip code; I do not own property; I do not own a swimming pool. What I am is a happily married man with children and grandchildren. I am hardly a Bonny Lee Bakley target.

Now, if the Old Man had been alive during Bonny Lee Bakley's time, he may well have been on her list. He was not a hustler of women, but he could seldom say no to anything, let alone a proposition from a pretty woman. He was Tarzan. I'm a longshoreman. I invented the phrase "Joe Straight Arrow." Bonny simply got the wrong guy. It had to have been the imposter, or at least an imposter.

Fortunately, in July of 2001, *Entertainment Weekly* printed a retraction. With Diane's volunteer work helping transplant patients, it is imperative that both of us maintain a good public image. We cannot accept being associated with an immoral person such as Bonny Lee Bakley, or be even remotely associated with a high-profile Hollywood murder case. (Bonny was murdered, and her husband, Robert Blake, was eventually charged with the crime.) It's unthinkable.

The most annoying thing that I encounter are guys who say to me, "You ain't Johnny Weissmuller Jr. I met him. He's about five-eight and 180 pounds. He sure as hell ain't no six-six and 220 pounds!" What can I say?

TARZOON

Although I am embarrassed to mention it, I suppose I should cover my experience with the production of *Tarzoon*. This took place just before I married Diane. Better you hear it from me than from my detractors.

Edgar Rice Burroughs Incorporated sued a film company in France for releasing a cartoon parody of Tarzan titled *Shame of the Jungle*. The French company won the lawsuit because parody, to almost any degree, is permissible under French law. One of the film's producers, after visiting the United States during these legal proceedings, commented, "Once I talked to the persons in the United States, I came to realize that a parody of Tarzan by us was like a parody of Jeanne D'Arc by them. Tarzan was, apparently, a national treasure. We printed the film anyway, of course, although we did have to change the name of the film to *Tarzoon.*"

Unfortunately, in an unthinking moment, I became involved in that mess, along with John Belushi and Bill Murray of *Saturday Night Live.* They had asked Dad to do a voice-over for this spoof, and he didn't want to do it because he was ashamed to. It certainly wouldn't be a hit with his Tarzan fans. As usual, when he needed a way out of a difficult situation, he pulled me out of the wings on a tether. He told them that he couldn't do it, but he had just the guy who could. Nobody's old man is perfect, I'm sure, but that is one failing of Dad's that I found hard to forgive. He had absolutely no compunction about using me as a patsy when he wanted to run away from something and still please everybody.

In a weak and foolish moment (I guess I was tempted by the chance to work with Belushi and Murray), I agreed. The gig paid only three thousand dollars, and to this day I regret having done the damned thing. The French producers said it would never be released in the United States, but they later sold it to some guy in New York, who publicized the hell out of it, with Johnny Weissmuller Jr. receiving top billing. They wanted to milk the Weissmuller name. Still later, they wanted me to reloop it, but I refused.

That's when María and Lisa jumped on the bandwagon and sold a story to the *National Enquirer* that was printed under the headline "**Father Too Ill to Be Told of Son's Shameful Porno Flick!**" Mother was furious with me, and with María and Lisa. Diane's mother read that headline in the supermarket, and she called Diane to ask how she could explain to Diane's father this thing about his son-in-law to be. I don't think she ever told him. But it never really went away. To this day, every time I'm interviewed, *Tarzoon* is the first thing I'm asked about.

HOWARD STERN

In 1997, Diane and I flew to New York City to do some promotion work for American Movie Classics. AMC is a twenty-four-hour cable network devoted to the Golden Age of Hollywood, and it's beamed into sixty-three million homes nationwide. All AMC films are presented as they were originally intended to be seen: uncut, uninterrupted, commercial-free, and without colorization. Diane and I love it; so does Howard Stern.

Stern is also a big Tarzan fan, so much so that when AMC launched a three-day marathon of Tarzan movies and documentaries, he stocked up on food and drink and spent an entire weekend holed up in his house, watching Tarzan swing from vine to vine. In his loud and clear voice, Stern informed anybody and everybody that there was only one real Tarzan, and that, in his humble estimation, was Johnny Weissmuller.

Diane heard this, told producer Sal Cataldi about it, and soon an interview with "the son of Tarzan" was arranged on Stern's radio show. I was nervous about that, and I fully expected to come out tattered and torn, as did almost all of Stern's guests. Not so. We talked about the Mia Farrow–Woody Allen scandal (which was causing a world tempest, but scarcely a Hollywood ripple), and Howard lacerated a few other people before proceeding to a discussion of my father and me. Apparently, Howard Stern really loved my father as Tarzan, and he was the most cordial and respectful host that I have ever worked with. Cataldi called me and said that he could not believe how well the show went. It was the first time he had heard Howard be that nice to anyone.

BLACK TARZAN

Many blacks, to this day, resent the fact that Tarzan was not represented by Edgar Rice Burroughs and Hollywood as a black person. Or that his Jane was not a black Jane. In the film *Investigating Tarzan*, a black girl says, "Tarzan should have been a black man, not that Johnny . . . that swimmer guy . . . whatever his name is . . . sort of a fantasy of white people, I guess." A black man says, "A white guy in the jungles of Africa, killing animals and black men with abandon? Conquers all that he sees, destroys what he likes. . . . We are to believe this crap? I am . . . well . . . I guess you might say . . . insulted."

In the same documentary, France Zobada, a black actress who later worked on the *Sheena, Queen of the Jungle* films, was pro and con. She liked the Tarzan series because "they were the first films in which we saw, as children, a man who could speak with animals." But she did not like the elements of racism inherent in the Edgar Rice Burroughs novels. France Zobada went on to say,

> When they called me to play in the Sheena film, I was very excited. I thought that I would be a she-Tarzan. Not so. I discovered that the mind-set of the day prohibited a black she-Tarzan. I was, instead, cast as a black villainess . . . well, it was good money, and I accepted the role anyway. . . . But what confuses me to this day is the fact that Tarzan waited most of his adult life, without sex, for a white princess to drop from the sky. . . . Are we to believe that he did not take a black woman from the jungle in all that time? . . . The new Tarzan image must be one of brotherhood rather than paternalism.

My own feelings on this subject are best expressed by Professor E.B. Holtsmark, Department of Classics, University of Iowa:

What Burroughs did is really fascinating. Tarzan embodies the mythical imagination, really, of Western civilization. He is clearly based on characters from ancient mythology. Search for a woman, quest for knowledge, search for treasure . . . these are all things that you find in the *Odyssey*. . . . There is this element of racism in the novels, [but] you cannot judge the past by present standards, whether in literature or anything else. I do not approve of sexism in the Bible. I think that there are sequences of intolerable, unspeakable violence in Homer's poetry, but I don't see that as a reason to reject Homer—or Burroughs's novels . . . the Tarzan stories, I think, have the ability to speak to all ages and—really—all time.

There *is* a magic in the Tarzan films—something that transcends race, color, bias. Peter Elliott is an actor who worked on *Greystoke*, the 1984 Tarzan film; he also studied the species of primates who, in the first Burroughs Tarzan novel, raised a human baby as one of their own. Elliott comes close to describing that magic: "Tarzan represents the famous 'missing link' between primate animals and human animals. I sometimes wonder if the universal appeal of Tarzan is that he somehow articulates this notion of bridging these two different worlds. . . . I think we all crave contact, somehow, with our real animal selves."

Perhaps. Perhaps not. But I do know that Tarzan is Tarzan. Try to change his color at this late date, have him mutter political slogans or other such nonsense, and you might wind up inciting a revolution. And I firmly believe that for an earlier generation of young people, watching Tarzan movies was a far less hazardous activity than hanging around on street corners, looking for a mark to hit or a customer to buy your drugs or guns—a lifestyle to which some of today's young are susceptible.

THE EDGAR RICE BURROUGHS CLUBS

ERB clubs span the globe. The guiding force behind them is Danton Burroughs, the grandson of Edgar Rice Burroughs. I doubt that anyone can calculate how many hundreds of thousands of admirers of Edgar Rice Burroughs there are, people who assiduously collect every bit of trivia concerning the author's life. It is almost a cult. One Burroughs admirer, George McWhorter, even goes so far as to say, "I think that Edgar Rice Burroughs is probably the greatest undiscovered national treasure of the United States of America. . . . There have been a total of 164 different fan magazines devoted to Edgar Rice Burroughs. I don't think that [even] Sherlock Holmes can claim that."

Perhaps this is a little strong. There are still plenty of people whose idea of Tarzan and his origins is pretty vague. One lady, a native of Tarzana, California, where Burroughs once lived, and which was named after his Tarzan, replied when asked if she knew why her town was so named, "Oh, sure! Tarzan, who was named after Edgar Allen . . . ?"

Edgar Rice Burroughs himself, when asked how he came to write *Tarzan of the Apes*, replied, "I had the story from one who had no business telling it to me—or to any other. I do not say that the story is true, but the fact that in telling it to you, I have taken fictitious names for the principal characters quite sufficiently evidences the sincerity of my own belief that it may be true."

There is no doubt that readers all over the world wanted the tale to be true. Few stories have ever captured the public imagination so thoroughly. And few have been so lucrative. Edgar Rice Burroughs was tired of being poor, and he took steps to ensure that he would never be poor again. In the words of his biographer, John Taliaferro, "[Burroughs] was ahead of his time in the area of intellectual property, in negotiating First Rights, Secondary Rights, merchandising . . . there were costumes . . . dolls . . . comic strips. . . . He took a resource, Tarzan, and squeezed every drop out of it possible."

The 1930s were good years for Edgar Rice Burroughs. He'd come a long way since 1912, when the first installment of *Tarzan of the Apes* came out in the October issue of *All-Story* magazine, which sold for fifteen cents. But in the 1940s, the Tarzan novels "lost ground," writes Marianna Torgovnick, in an article titled "Taking Tarzan Seriously." She quotes *Life* magazine's Paul Mandel as saying that this occurred "because substantial clans of American boys had started living their own real-life jungle dramas" in the Pacific arena during World War II. Torgovnick continues:

> By 1960, only nine of the twenty-three novels remained in print. . . . Biographies of Burroughs and the essays by Mandel and Vidal [Gore Vidal, writing for *Esquire*] state clearly—too clearly—the reason for Tarzan's return. Burroughs's fans, the explanations go, always wanted Tarzan in paperback, Burroughs's heirs, unlike Burroughs himself, became complacent in the decade after his death with regard to sales and profit.
>
> When the fans discovered that Burroughs's heirs had sloppily allowed copyrights to lapse, they urged publishers to reprint, and the publishers did. The rest is publishing history, and history of an unusual kind in that the audience created the demand and the occasion for the reprints, not the publishing houses. . . .

Some of Burroughs's heirs may have dropped the ball in the past, but Danton Burroughs is apparently a chip off the old block. He holds regular meetings in his grandfather's house in Tarzana, hosting ERB club members from all over the world. Celebrities such as Maureen O'Sullivan (who died at the age of eighty-seven in 1998), former Tarzan Denny Miller, and former Sheena Tanya Roberts often attend, as do Tarzan and Edgar Rice Burroughs aficionados and merchandisers. Artifacts and memorabilia of every description are sold, bartered, or exchanged at these gatherings.

And, in Danton's words, "We are very protective of the Burroughs copyrights. Unauthorized Tarzan films are regularly produced in such places as Singapore, Czechoslovakia, India; and we sue whenever and wherever possible." Witness the aforementioned lawsuit over *Tarzoon*.

As I mentioned earlier in this book, Edgar Rice Burroughs was disturbed about the Hollywood treatment of Tarzan. He became so upset that he started his own film company and chose his own Tarzan—named Herman Brix, who was slim like an Olympic runner and very elegant. Dressed in a dinner jacket, Brix truly looked like an English lord. Although he played the role from 1935 to 1938, Brix never really caught on. Still, others tried to emulate his approach.

Gradually, the image evolved. Gordon Scott, who played Tarzan from 1955 to 1960, commented, "There was an effort [in my era] to restore the Tarzan image to something more akin to the manner in which Edgar Rice Burroughs had portrayed [Tarzan] in the original *Ape Man*—a multilingual, more sophisticated Tarzan." Director Hugh Hudson, with *Greystoke, the Legend of Tarzan* (1984), starring Christopher Lambert, probably came closest to pulling off this new Tarzan image, but that image just didn't catch on with the public.

A Johnny Weissmuller Filmography

(Courtesy of Geoff St. Andrews)
Films featuring a cameo appearance by Johnny Weissmuller have been omitted from this filmography. They are documented in countless other publications.

Crystal Champions (1929, Paramount) This Grantland Rice short featured Weissmuller and other Olympic water champions at the famous Silver Springs in Florida, which would serve as a location for underwater scenes in *Tarzan Finds a Son!*

Tarzan the Ape Man (1932, MGM) Johnny Weissmuller in his first appearance as Tarzan.

Tarzan and His Mate (1934, MGM)

Tarzan Escapes (1936, MGM)

Tarzan Finds a Son! (1939, MGM) Johnny Sheffield makes his initial appearance as Tarzan's adopted son.

Tarzan's Secret Treasure (1941, MGM)

Tarzan's New York Adventure (1942, MGM)

Tarzan Triumphs (1943, RKO)

Tarzan's Desert Mystery (1943, RKO)

Tarzan and the Amazons (1945, RKO)

Swamp Fire (1946, Paramount)

Tarzan and the Leopard Woman (1946, RKO)

Tarzan and the Huntress (1947, RKO)

Tarzan and the Mermaids (1948, RKO)

Jungle Jim (1948, Columbia)

The Lost Tribe (1949, Columbia)

Mark of the Gorilla (1950, Columbia)

Captive Girl (1950, Columbia) Four swimmers in this one: Weissmuller, Buster Crabbe, Anita Lhoest, and Rusty Wescoatt.

Pygmy Island (1950, Columbia)

Fury of the Congo (1951, Columbia)

Jungle Manhunt (1951, Columbia)

Jungle Jim in the Forbidden Land (1952, Columbia)

Voodoo Tiger (1952, Columbia)

Savage Mutiny (1953, Columbia)

Valley of Head Hunters (1953, Columbia)

Killer Ape (1953, Columbia)

Jungle Man-Eaters (1954, Columbia)

Cannibal Attack (1954, Columbia) For the final three films on this list, Johnny played himself, since Screen Gems now owned the rights to the Jungle Jim character.

Jungle Moon Men (1955, Columbia)

Devil Goddess (1955, Columbia)

Devil Goddess was Johnny Weissmuller's last Katzman film for Columbia. Then followed a twenty-six-episode Jungle Jim TV series for Screen Gems. It's a pity that it couldn't go on forever. After that, out of work, with no more jungles to conquer, it was only a downhill swing for Johnny Weissmuller.

The Jungle Jim TV Series

In 1954, the screen rights to the Jungle Jim character were turned over to Columbia's subsidiary, Screen Gems. At Screen Gems, producer Harold Greene was given the opportunity to do for television what Sam Katzman had done for the movies. By further lowering the budgets and by using as much stock footage as possible, Greene made a success of the project.

When Johnny Weissmuller completed his final film for Columbia, he did the TV series for Screen Gems. The series costarred Martin Huston as Weissmuller's son and Norman Fredric as his friend Kaseem. It says something about Weissmuller's enduring appeal that the series lasted as long as it did. It was never designed for prime time, and it went almost immediately into syndication, but it kept the Jungle King clothed and fed for several more years.

Here is a list of *Jungle Jim* episode titles:

Man Killer
Land of Terror
Treasure of the Amazon
Lagoon of Death
A Fortune in Ivory
Jungle Justice
The Eyes of Manobo
The King's Ghost
White Magic
The Deadly Idol
The Leopard's Paw
The Man from Zanzibar
Precious Cargo
The Golden Parasol
Code of the Jungle
Wild Man of the Jungle
Safari into Danger
Blood Money
Striped Fury
The Sacred Scarab
Voodoo Drums
The Avenger
Return of the Tauregs

The Silver Locket
Gift of Evil (a.k.a. Jungle Fever)
Power of Darkness

Johnny Weissmuller Swimming Records

Weissmuller participated in fifty-two national championships (thirty-six individual and sixteen relay team) and sixty-seven world championships. He set fifty-one individual world records, achieved ninety-four individual American records, and was a member of thirteen American record-setting relay teams (between 1921 and 1928). He was also a member of national championship water polo teams in 1924 and 1927.

Olympic Gold Medals

1924 (Paris, France)
100-meters freestyle
400-meters freestyle
800-meters United States relay team

1928 (Amsterdam, Holland)
100-meters freestyle
800-meters United States relay team

National Championships
(Outdoor)

(Event)	(Year)	(Time)
50 yards	1921	23.2
50 yards	1922	23.0
100 yards	1922	52.8
100 yards	1923	54.6
100 yards	1925	52.0

(Event)	(Year)	(Time)
100 meters	1926	59.6
100 meters	1927	58.0
100 meters	1928	57.8
220 yards	1921	2:28.0
220 yards	1922	2:22.4
440 yards	1922	5:16.4
440 yards	1923	5:37.4
440 yards	1925	5:22.5
440 yards	1926	5:21.8
440 yards	1927	4:52.0
440 yards	1928	4:58.6

(Indoor)

50 yards	1923	23.6
50 yards	1924	24.0
50 yards	1925	23.2
100 yards	1922	54.0
100 yards	1923	54.8
100 yards	1924	53.8
100 yards	1925	52.2
100 yards	1927	51.4
100 yards	1928	50.8
pentathlon	1922	
pentathlon	1923 (tied)	
220 yards	1922	2:17.4
220 yards	1923	2:22.0
220 yards	1924	2:14.8
220 yards	1927	2:10.8
220 yards	1928	2:10.4
500 yards	1922	5:46.8
500 yards	1923	5:43.6
500 yards	1924	5:50.4
500 yards	1927	5:28.4
500 yards	1928	5:35.0
50 yards (backstroke)	1923	1:42.0

Johnny Weissmuller Jr. Stage, Film, and Television Credits

STAGE

We're No Angels; *Yellow Jackets*; *Bus Stop*; *Hairy Ape*; *Under the Yum Yum Tree*; *Mr. Roberts*; *The Cain Mutiny Court Martial*; *Harvey*; *One Flew over the Cuckoo's Nest*; *That Splendid Little War*; *What the Devil*.

MOTION PICTURES

Andy Hardy Comes Home (MGM); *THX 1138* (American Zoetrope); *American Graffiti* (Zoetrope); *Magnum Force* (Warner Malpaiso); *Blackbird* (Columbia); *Massive Retaliation* (Massive Prod./Indep.); *Ewoks: The Battle for Endor* (Kerner Prod.); *Wildfire* (Indep.).

FILMS FOR TELEVISION

Kansas City Massacre (ABC); *Return to Manzanar*; *Alcatraz: The Whole Shocking Story* (Burbank); *The Johnnie Mae Gibson Story* (CBS); *Six against the Rock* (ABC).

TELEVISION SERIES

Sugarfoot; *Lawman*; *Outlaw*; *Death Valley Days*; *Wagon Train*; *Gunsmoke*; *Streets of San Francisco*; *Bert D'Angelo: Superstar*; *Alison Sydney Harrison* (pilot); *Tales of the Unexpected*; *Partners in Crime*.

COMMERCIALS

Ford Motor Company; American Motors; National Biscuit Company; Busch Beer.

Sources

Azcárraga, Gabriel. Tape recording, 2000.
Baxter, John. *Stunt: The Story of the Great Movie Stuntmen*. London: Macdonald, 1973.
Bogle, Donald. *Blacks in American Films and Television: An Encyclopedia*. New York: Simon and Schuster, 1988.
Essoe, Gabe. *Tarzan of the Movies*. New York: Cadillac, 1968.

Fury, David. *Johnny Weissmuller: Twice the Hero.* Minneapolis: Artist's Press, 2000.

——. *Kings of the Jungle: An Illustrated Reference to Tarzan on Screen and Television.* Jefferson: McFarland, 1994.

Gallery, Don. Interview, 2002.

Huston, John. Tape recording, 1978.

Jewell, Richard B. *The RKO Story.* London: Octopus Books, 1982.

Libby, Bill. "Tarzan Today: The Messed-Up Life of Johnny Weissmuller." *Saga* Jan. 1965.

McClelland, Allene Gates Weissmuller. Tape recordings, 1999.

Mueller, Arlene. "Hot Stove." *Sports Illustrated* 6 Aug. 1984.

Oliver, Mike. Tape recordings, 2000.

Olsen, Carolyn Roos. Tape recording, 2002.

Onyx, Narda. *Water, World, and Weissmuller.* Los Angeles: Vion, 1964.

Porges, Irwin. *Edgar Rice Burroughs: The Man Who Created Tarzan.* New York: Ballantine, 1975.

Silva, Maru Eugenia. Tape recording, 2000.

Weissmuller, Diane. Tape recordings, 1999–2002.

Weissmuller, Johnny, and Clarence A. Bush. *Swimming the American Crawl.* Cambridge: Houghton Mifflin; Riverside, 1930.

INDEX

Kahanamoku, Duke 36, 40
Kananamoku, Samuel 36, 40
Katzman, Sam 124
Keaton, Buster 92
Kennedy, Ted 201
Kohner, Paul 63
Konigshofer, Jon 86, 183, 185, 193
Kruger, Stubby 35, 45–46, 131, 159
Lake, A.P. (Artie) 156
Lake, Arthur 156
Lake, Patty (née Hearst) 96, 156
Lamas, Fernando 105, 106
Lambert, Christopher 218
Lanier, Toni 57–58
LaShelle, Art 78, 167
Lesser, Sol 41, 42, 94, 113
Lewis, Ted 51
Libby, Bill quoted 34
Life 217
London, Julie 156–57
Los Angeles Daily Times 124
Los Angeles Herald Express 109
Louis, Joe 181
MacMurray, Fred 108, 147
Mandel, Paul quoted 217
Mannix, Eddie 57
Marx Brothers 64
Matt's Bomba Movie Guide 82
Mature, Victor 150
Mayer, Louis B. 62, 64, 155
Mayne, Arlo 195
McGillivray, Perry 33, 35
McKim, Josephine 61
McWhorter, George quoted 13, quoted 216
Meany, Helen 45
Meuller, Arlene 118
MGM (Metro Goldwyn Mayer) Studios 54, 55–56, 57, 61, 62–64, 84, 87, 90, 94, 127, 153, 155, 168
Miller, Denny 218
Mitchum, Jimmy 141, 142–43, 153, 160
Mitchum, Robert 141, 143, 201
Mommie Dearest 154

Monroe, Marilyn 64
Morgan, Dennis 135
Moulin Rouge 201
Murray, Bill 214
Music Box Review, The 71
Nasser, Gamal Abdel 117
National Enquirer 15, 195, 196, 201, 214
Nelson, Ricky 153
New York Times quoted 33–34, 38
Norelius, Martha 45
Oakie, Jack 85
Oberon, Merle 107
Odyssey, The 216
Oliver, Mike quoted 106, 113, quoted 114, 152, 190, quoted 191, 193, 203
Oliver, Rita 193, 203
Olsen, Carolyn Roos quoted 100–102, quoted 138–39, quoted 149–51
O'Neal, Blackie 152
O'Neal, Patrick ("Ryan") 152–53
One Flew over the Cuckoo's Nest 183
On the Waterfront 176
Onyx, Narda quoted 30
O'Sullivan, Maureen 11, 58, quoted 60–62, quoted 70, 218
Parades, Eustasio Ordaz 211
Parsons, Harriet 107
Parsons, Louella quoted 119
Pitts, ZaSu 154
"Precious Gem Called Beryl, A" 212
Presley, Elvis 153
Previn, Andre 157
Queen Elizabeth II 181
Queen Wilhelmina 42–43, 81
Rambo 116
Ramond, Harald 100–102
Rathbone, Henry Riggs quoted 38
Raymond, Jim 174
Red Badge of Courage, The 64
Reed, W. Craig 15
Reed, William 15, 62, 100, 116, 179
Reynolds, Burt 153